CRIMINAL
INVESTIGATIONS

CYBERCRIME

CRIMINAL INVESTIGATIONS

CRIMINAL
INVESTIGATIONS

CYBERCRIME

JEFFREY IAN ROSS, PH.D.

CONSULTING EDITOR: **JOHN L. FRENCH**,

CRIME SCENE SUPERVISOR,
BALTIMORE POLICE CRIME LABORATORY

CHELSEA HOUSE
PUBLISHERS

An imprint of Infobase Publishing

CRIMINAL INVESTIGATIONS: Cybercrime

Chelsea House
An imprint of Infobase Publishing
132 West 31st Street
New York NY 10001

Library of Congress Cataloging-in-Publication Data
Ross, Jeffrey Ian.
Cybercrime / Jeffrey Ian Ross.
p. cm. — (Criminal investigations)
Includes bibliographical references and index.
ISBN-13: 978-0-7910-9406-8 (hardcover : alk. paper)
ISBN-10: 0-7910-9406-5 (hardcover : alk. paper)
1. Computer crimes. 2. Internet. I. Title. II. Series.
HV6773.R67 2010   364.16'8—dc22
                2009018860

Chelsea House books are available at special discounts when purchased
in bulk quantities for businesses, associations, institutions,
or sales promotions. Please call our Special Sales Department
in New York at (212) 967-8800 or (800) 322-8755.

You can find Chelsea House on the World Wide Web at
http://www.chelseahouse.com

Text design by Erika K. Arroyo
Cover design by Ben Peterson

Cover: Criminals often use the Internet to commit crimes
at a distance, while remaining anonymous.

Printed in the United States of America

Bang EJB 10 9 8 7 6 5 4 3 2 1

This book is printed on acid-free paper.

All links and Web addresses were checked and verified to be
correct at the time of publication. Because of the dynamic nature
of the Web, some addresses and links may have changed
since publication and may no longer be valid.

Contents

Acknowledgments

I want to thank many people who have assisted me along the way. Thanks to Jake Elwell, for being an excellent literary agent and for bringing this project to my attention; James Chambers, Chelsea House Publishers, for being an excellent editor; Catherine Leidemer for cleaning up my prose; John French, the consulting editor, for his patience; Chipp Jones, of Computerchipp, Washington, DC for periodic technical advice; and Kelley Ellsworth, director of Byte Back, a nonprofit organization, based in Washington, DC, that helps lower income individuals improve their computer skills, for providing a public forum for me to test some of the ideas contained in this book. And finally to my family, Natasha, Keanu and Dakota for tolerating my divided attention.

This book is dedicated to Ruy Cabrera, my brother-in-law, of Digital Design Systems, who has helped me out of more computer jams than I care to remember.

Foreword

In 2000 there were 15,000 murders in the United States. During that same year about a half million people were assaulted, 1.1 million cars were stolen, 400,000 robberies took place, and more than 2 million homes and businesses were broken into. All told, in the last year of the twentieth century, there were more than 11 million crimes committed in this country.*

In 2000 the population of the United States was approximately 280 million people. If each of the above crimes happened to a separate person, only 4 percent of the country would have been directly affected. Yet everyone is in some way affected by crime. Taxes pay patrolmen, detectives, and scientists to investigate it, lawyers and judges to prosecute it, and correctional officers to watch over those convicted of committing it. Crimes against businesses cause prices to rise as their owners pass on the cost of theft and security measures installed to prevent future losses. Tourism in cities, and the money it brings in, may rise and fall in part due to stories about crime in their streets. And every time someone is shot, stabbed, beaten, or assaulted, or when someone is jailed for having committed such a crime, not only they suffer but so may their friends, family, and loved ones. Crime affects everyone.

It is the job of the police to investigate crime with the purpose of putting the bad guys in jail and keeping them there, hoping thereby to punish past crimes and discourage new ones. To accomplish this, a police officer has to be many things: dedicated, brave, smart, honest, and imaginative. Luck helps, but it's not required. And there's one more virtue that should be associated with law enforcement. A good police officer is patient.

Patience is a virtue in crime fighting because police officers and detectives know something that most criminals don't. It's not a secret, but most lawbreakers don't learn it until it is too late. Criminals who make money robbing people, breaking into houses, or stealing cars; who live by dealing drugs or committing murder; who spend their days on the wrong side of the law, or commit any other crimes, must remember this: a criminal has to get away with every crime they commit. However, to get criminals off the street and put them behind bars, the police only have to catch a criminal once.

The methods by which police catch criminals are varied. Some are as old as recorded history and others are so new that they have yet to be tested in court. One of the first stories in the Bible is of murder, when Cain killed his brother Abel (Genesis 4:1–16). With few suspects to consider and an omniscient detective, this was an easy crime to solve. However, much later in that same work, a young man named Daniel steps in when a woman is accused of an immoral act by two elders (Daniel 13:1–63). By using the standard police practice of separating the witnesses before questioning them, he is able to arrive at the truth of the matter.

From the time of the Bible to almost present day, police investigations did not progress much further than questioning witnesses and searching the crime scene for obvious clues as to a criminal's identity. It was not until the late 1800s that science began to be employed. In 1879 the French began to use physical measurements and later photography to identify repeat offenders. In the same year a Scottish missionary in Japan used a handprint found on a wall to exonerate a man accused of theft. In 1892 a bloody fingerprint lead Argentine police to charge and convict a mother of killing her children, and by 1905 Scotland Yard had convicted several criminals thanks to this new science.

Progress continued. By the 1920s scientists were using blood analysis to determine if recovered stains were from the victim or suspect, and the new field of firearms examination helped link bullets to the guns which fired them.

Nowadays, things are even harder on criminals, when by leaving behind a speck of blood, dropping a sweat-stained hat, or even taking a sip from a can of soda, they can give the police everything they need to identify and arrest them.

In the first decade of the twenty-first century the main tools used by the police include

- questioning witnesses and suspects
- searching the crime scene for physical evidence
- employing informants and undercover agents
- investigating the whereabouts of previous offenders when a crime they've been known to commit has occurred
- matching evidence found on one crime scene to that found on others or to previously arrested suspects, using computer databases
- sharing information with other law enforcement agencies via the Internet
- using modern communications to keep the public informed and enlist their aid in ongoing investigations

But just as they have many different tools with which to solve crime, so too do they have many different kinds of crime and criminals to investigate. There is murder, kidnapping, and bank robbery. There are financial crimes committed by con men who gain their victim's trust, or computer experts who hack into computers. There are criminals who have formed themselves into gangs and those who are organized into national syndicates. And there are those who would kill as many people as possible, either for the thrill of taking a human life or in the horribly misguided belief that it will advance their cause.

The Criminal Investigation series looks at all of the above and more. Each book in the series takes one type of crime and gives the reader an overview of the history of the crime, the methods and motives behind it, the people who have committed it, and the means by which these people are caught and punished. In this series celebrity crimes will be discussed and exposed. Mysteries that have yet to be solved will be presented. Readers will discover the truth about murderers, serial killers, and bank robbers whose stories have become myths and legends. These books will explain how criminals can separate a person from his hard-earned cash, how they prey on the weak and helpless, what is being done to stop them, and what one can do to help prevent becoming a victim.

John L. French,
Crime Scene Supervisor,
Baltimore Police Crime Laboratory

* Federal Bureau of Investigation. "Uniform Crime Reports, Crime in the United States 2000." Available online. URL: http://www.fbi.gov/ucr/00cius.htm. Accessed January 11, 2008.

Introduction:
The Threat of Cybercrime

Some people are slow adopters of new technology. They aren't likely to investigate, rush out, and buy the latest electronic gadget or computer **software** that promises to make their work or life easier. These individuals were probably the most reluctant to buy DVD players and cell phones or to upgrade from WordPerfect to Microsoft Word; they may have been the last among their friends to use any type of computer that required a mouse.

What prompts this hesitance to accept technological advances is unclear. For older people it may be that having grown up in a simpler, less costly time, they learned their way around mechanical things. Their philosophy was that if something was broken, replace the faulty part; otherwise, run it into the ground. This is a strategy often based on frugality. If an old technology still works, some people see no need to switch to a new one. Or maybe these individuals have seen so many failed new inventions, like the ill-fated triangle shaped tablet computer, that they've become skeptical about new products, their manufacturers' claims, and the people who use them.

Yet many tech-savvy individuals do not hesitate to pre-order online or line up at a brick-and-mortar electronics store to purchase the latest high-tech device the day it's released to the public. Many people are technological junkies. They spend hours a day in front of a computer screen, using a personal data assistant (e.g., BlackBerry), or surfing the Web. But the information highway these people travel is not always a safe place for work or for play; many users have become victims of cybercrime. Certainly, this doesn't happen to everyone, but it does occur on a large-enough scale that most people have learned to be cautious every time they receive an e-mail from someone they don't know.

DEFINING CYBERCRIME

Among the many types of illegal acts that affect the average citizen is cybercrime. Although this phenomenon goes by a number of different names, including "crime by keyboard" and "information-technology" or "high-technology" crime, the general public is probably more familiar with its specific techniques such as hacking, phishing, Trojan horses, piracy, and virus distribution. Collectively, these practices "use computers and computer technology as tools in crime commission" including manipulating "information stored on computer systems," in such a "way that violates the law."[1] Although it is tempting to consider stealing computer equipment and software from a retail merchant as cybercrimes, these are best classified as thefts.

Based on cybercrime expert Samuel C. McQuade's research, cybercrime is defined as the "use of computers or other electronic devices via information systems to facilitate illegal behaviors."[2] Electronic devices include, but are not limited to, cell phones, scanners, fax machines, personal data assistants, and computers. By necessity it is a "broad label for technologically evolving forms of crime." Cybercrimes are now routine problems for computer users, the organizations they belong to or work for, and entire countries. By necessity everyone must constantly be vigilant about this kind of crime lest they fall victim to it.[3]

Cybercrime encompasses a range of illegal activities that share a common environment: electronic, digital, or cyberspace. The majority of cybercrimes are now carried out through the **Internet** or **World Wide Web**, which is a communication network that allows computer users to electronically communicate with each other. Criminologists and law enforcement experts see cybercrimes as a form of white-collar crime. If there is group of individuals who regularly engage in this activity, then it is considered similar to the methods of traditional organized crime groups, such as the Mafia. According to author Gina De Angelis, "Most computer crimes do not involve violence, but play on greed, pride, or some other character weakness of the victim. They are based on dishonesty, not force."[4]

Not surprisingly, it's possible to commit a wide range of crimes via the Web. These acts include, but are not limited to: information theft; illegally accessing information stored on computers, computer networks, or computer systems; damaging information stored on computers and computer systems; and deceptions that end in violent crimes. In many respects, these crimes aren't necessarily new; it's the way in which they're committed that's novel. This is why many experts consider cybercrimes a case of "old wine in new bottles."

This category of crime also includes actions the general public may not consider to be criminal, such as sharing or copying music and movies, which violates copyright laws. This is called "cyberpiracy," and it denies rightful compensation to the composer, musician, publisher, or other owner of the pirated works. This means a loss of revenue for musicians, actors, and other artists. That consequence rarely prevents tech-savvy people from file sharing: copying electronically saved files and giving or selling them to others.

A SHORT HISTORY OF CYBERCRIME

The history of cybercrime runs parallel to the development of the computer, **operating systems**, software development, and the Internet.

Brief history of computers. Computers and computer technology are pervasive in today's society. They allow people to accomplish many tasks at a fraction of the time and expense that they once cost. The earliest computers used vacuum tubes that, when properly assembled, filled a room. Over time, the manufacture, use, and prevalence of computers has increased, and their size and relative cost has decreased. Now they can fit in a wristwatch. People use mainframe supercomputers, desktop computers, laptops, and handhelds. Over time their prices have decreased and the kinds of tasks that they can perform have expanded. As computers have become more commonplace, the possibility of using them for criminal activities has increased.

In order for a computer to properly run, however, it needs an operating system and software.

Operating systems. An operating system is the structure or architecture of internal commands that allows software to run. It includes the kind of memory and commands that enable the software (also known as **applications**) installed on a computer to run. It also allows a computer to multitask (i.e., do different jobs at the same time). For example, when a user is listening to a radio station on the Internet and typing on the computer at the same time, this complex function is handled by the operating system. There are approximately 250 operating systems in use throughout the world. The two principle operating systems are Microsoft Windows and Apple Mac OS X. Others such as Linux and Unix are used mainly with large mainframe computers.

Software. In order for a computer to perform tasks, computer programs—or software—must be written. Programs have evolved and the languages used for computer programming have changed since the early days of computing. Programs are a sequence of logical steps, an ordered series of commands that enable the computer to carry out a user's demands. Software is used for many kinds of applications in the fields of accounting, communications, design, mechanics, etc. Software is sold by companies like Microsoft while other types are available free through organizations and their Web sites. Some free software is sponsored by the Free Software Foundation, the GNU Project, and the Mozilla Foundation.

The Internet. Since the 1990s the Internet has pervaded the lives of people who live in the Western world and in advanced industrialized countries. But this was not always the case. The Internet originated in the 1960s with a system called the Advanced Research Projects Agency Network (ARPANET). It was designed by the United States military to enhance communications should existing mechanisms fail during a nuclear attack. "The creation of the network entailed the development not only of the appropriate computer **hardware**, but also of 'protocols,' the codes and rules that would allow different computers to 'understand' each other. . . . By 1969 the ARPANET was up and running, initially linking together a handful of university research communities with government agencies."[5]

In 1970 the military released ARPANET to the American-based National Science Foundation. Also during that year, scientists at the European Organization for Nuclear Research (CERN) physics laboratory in Switzerland developed the first Web browser. The original ARPANET then joined the U.S. Department of Defense with four California universities and the University of Utah. In 1971 the network added Harvard University, Massachusetts Institute of Technology, and the National Aeronautics and Space Administration. Starting around 1973, users started using it as a mechanism to communicate with each other beyond its original intent to enhance communications surrounding computational services. Eventually other countries and computer systems joined with the ARPANET and a system of network protocols, a mechanism to recognize senders and receivers, was developed.

Recognition is typically done through a specific number or code attached to each computer system or **server**. New versions of the protocols were developed to allow more complex text messages and the sharing of images. Today most computer users take for granted hardware, such as **modems** and **routers**, and software, like Web browsers, that facilitate this kind of communication. One of the most popular Web browsers in use today is Microsoft's Internet Explorer. Approximately 80 percent of Internet usage takes place in the United States.

David S. Wall, a British expert, argues that the history of cybercrime can be divided into three distinct stages. The first is traditional or ordinary crimes, in which criminals use computers to gather information to commit crimes. Next are hybrid cybercrimes, which refers to using the Internet to commit traditional crimes. Third, true cybercrimes, are cases in which the computer is used for crime. This includes behaviors such as phishing or hacking. Now a new generation of cybercrime involves a loose allegiance among spammers, **hackers,** and virus writers to gain access to computers and computer systems.[6]

One of the first recorded incidents of cybercrime can be traced back to 1958 when a Minneapolis bank employee was able to change bank records so that, over time, he would receive a rather large sum of money. This technique, called "salami slicing," allows perpetrators to take out a small amount of money from his or her victims' accounts so the withdrawals are barely noticeable. Add together the money taken over time and it becomes a respectable amount of cash.

Since then, the kinds of criminal activities one could do with the assistance of a computer have increased. In 1996, during a conference sponsored by the United States Department of Justice, 10 computer-crime-related terms were identified, including: technological crime, high-tech crime, economic crime, technology-based crime, new age crime, computer and Internet-related crime, computer-assisted crime, digital crime, electronic crime, and Internet crime. According to McQuade:

> Cybercrime is now the term most often used to label activities in which perpetrators use computers or other electronic IT devices via information systems to facilitate illegal behaviors. In essence, cybercrime involves using electronic gadgets to access, control, manipulate, or use data for illegal purposes. IT devices now used to commit crimes include desktop, laptop and minicomputers, as well as cell phones, PDAs, fax machines, digital cameras, voice recorders, scanners, and so on.[7]

Finally, one of the greatest catalysts for cybercrimes has been the development of electronic or e-business and e-commerce. As this sector of the economy has increased, so too have the opportunities for cybercriminals to exploit these systems. Additionally, since the widespread adoption and use of computers in business, important information that is stored on these machines has been compromised.[8] Personal information such as Social Security numbers, health information, academic grades, and so on are at risk of exposure to theft.

What Is Cybercrime?

Before the invention of the cell phone; the Internet; deep-discount, long-distance calling programs and cards; and Skype (a free Web-based service that allows users to talk long distance with other subscribers via the Internet), a band of urban outlaws called **phreakers** developed. They broke into telephone carriers' systems and made free long-distance calls, not just in the United States but around the world. One of the most well-known phreakers is John T. Draper. During the early 1970s, Draper discovered that by blowing into the phone at the right time with a toy whistle, which was given away free in boxes of Captain Crunch cereal, he was able to access the telephone lines as if he were a telephone operator. Not only did Draper sell this information to others, but he constructed a "blue box" that made hooking up to the phone lines all that much easier. It wasn't long before Draper came to the attention of the authorities. He was arrested, convicted of wire fraud, and sentenced to federal prison.

Because cybercrime depends on the invention of new digital technology, the possibility for innovative kinds of cybercrime grows as new electronic gadgets with computer processing capability are invented, manufactured, sold to the public, and purchased by consumers. Some cybercrime experts have long laundry lists of actions that they consider to be cybercrime. With the invention of new electronic machines, these lists grow.

John T. Draper, also known as Captain Crunch because he used toy whistles found in boxes of the popular cereal to commit wire fraud, answers questions during an interview in October 1976. *AP Photo*

COMPUTER ASSISTED AND FACILITATED CRIMES

Like other types of crime, cybercrimes can vary in severity. Some of the relatively low-impact actions sometimes classified as cyber-crimes (but which many security professionals don't consider cybercrimes at all) include purchasing items from different states or countries where they are legal and having them shipped to a place where the item is illegal, or purchasing items from another region to avoid or save on taxes. The latter is particularly true in the case of cigarettes, alcohol, and legal drugs, where purchasers can save a substantial amount of money.

Another instance of computer-assisted crime is called "click fraud." Many Web sites, particularly ones that are news or media related, including popular blogs, derive income for their owners, or a substantial part of their revenue, from advertising that is placed alongside their content. Thus, a large measure of a site's worth is contingent upon advertisers believing that the site receives considerable traffic and gets a lot of "hits," or user views. To beef up statistics, some unscrupulous Web site operators may pay people to visit their site numerous times each day, thereby pushing up the statistics and duping potential or actual advertis-ers into believing that the site receives more traffic than it actu-ally does.

Also, most Internet users are familiar with spam, which is unsolicited and usually unwelcome advertisements for all kinds of products, from music purchases to Viagra. While annoying, spam is not illegal, unless it promotes an illegal product or service. Spam-ming occurs when marketing firms or departments of companies send out thousands of similar e-mail messages at the same time. Typically, spam is prevented through software that can block this type of e-mail. Some people appreciate these e-mails, especially if they are from preferred vendors, offer discounts on purchases, or alert recipients of current or impending sales on merchandise or services.

Users may be targeted for spam because of the Web sites they visit or because they gave their e-mail address to sites and failed to check the box indicating that it should not be shared with other vendors. There are many other ways that merchandisers can harvest e-mail addresses. "Through the use of tracking cookies and images, spam may be designed so that by merely opening up the message, your computer is identified as belonging to a potential customer, thus resulting in more spam being sent to you."[1]

TYPES OF CYBERCRIME

"One of the most important areas of Internet usage relates to its applications in electronic business or e-commerce. Businesses increasingly use the Internet as a routine part of their activities, ranging from research and development, to production, distribution, marketing and sales. These uses create a range of criminal opportunities—for example, the theft of trade secrets and sensitive strategic information. . ., the distribution of online selling systems, and the fraudulent use of credit cards to obtain goods and services."[2] Important personal information that resides on these mainframes and can be stolen includes Social Security numbers, health information, grades, and so on.

Many crimes now committed via the Internet are not necessarily new. They are modifications or sophisticated versions of fraud, theft, trespassing, and property destruction that use a new technology: the computer and the Internet. Following are the most serious forms of cybercrime.

Intellectual property theft/theft of proprietary information. Periodically, individuals obtain unauthorized access to companies' internal computers (called "hacking") and steal proprietary information (also known as trade secrets). This information is then used by competitors to build, create, or sell their own products or services. In many respects, this is a sophisticated kind of corporate espionage.

Illegal copying of software, music, and motion pictures. Copying software, unlike other kinds of media, usually does not result in any loss of quality. The copy is as good as the original. Software is typically copied for its functionality, not its appearance. Software producers claim that pirated software costs them billions of dollars they might otherwise earn through sales of their product. In addition to software, music CDs and video DVDs are also illegally copied, with similar economic impact on the recording and movie industries.

Hacking. This involves the illegal and unauthorized access by an outsider to an individual's e-mail account or personal computer, or an organization's computer system. This crime is a modern form of trespassing.

Distribution of malware. This includes computer viruses, Trojan horses, and worms. A virus is a piece of undetected malicious computer code that attaches itself to computer files. This can result in the deletion of important files and prevent a computer from working properly. It is typically spread when the malware attaches itself to an individual's e-mail contact list and is subsequently sent to the entire list. Other viruses are sent through attachments. Worms take advantage of weaknesses in security programs and other software to attack a computer. A Trojan horse is a program that appears harmless, but secretly attacks an affected computer.

Identity theft. With this particular crime, an individual or criminal organization usually gets access to someone's bank account or credit card information and starts spending that person's money or charging merchandise to his or her credit card or bank account. The kinds of personal information and the situations in which criminals can make use of this information are almost limitless.

Phishing. This deception is an attempt to lure unsuspecting computer users to phony Web sites that mimic the sites of legitimate businesses or public or government organizations. These copycat sites trick users into revealing private and sensitive information such as their usernames, passwords, and account numbers. This information is then used by or sent to criminals.

Cyberstalking and cyberbullying. The Internet and instant messaging (IM) have made it much easier to contact, harass, and threaten others. The problems of cyberstalking and cyberbullying are not limited to infatuated or disgruntled fans of musicians, actors, and politicians. Via the Internet it is now possible for the general public to track down the home, business, and e-mail addresses of countless individuals. This problem has worsened due not only to Web sites that provide company or organizational telephone and personnel directories, but also to blogs and social networking sites such as Facebook, Friendster, MySpace, and LinkedIn, which make personal information accessible on the Web.

Online pornography and prostitution. The Internet has made possible the transmission of pornography of all types and has made it easier for individuals who want to obtain the services of a prostitute to do so.

REPORTING CYBERCRIME

Despite news media accounts claiming that crime in general is increasing, and regardless of the numerous movies and television series that use cybercrime as a plot device, most seasoned criminologists and law enforcement professionals realize that there are several problems with measuring crime in general and cybercrime in particular. These difficulties mainly involve the reliability of primary data collection efforts. There are three major ways crime data is collected: through police reports, victimization studies, and self-reports. Each has its advantages and disadvantages.

Sources of cybercrime statistics typically come from databases or surveys administered by law enforcement organizations at the federal, state, and local level, other government agencies, and the private sector. In some cases government and private agencies have partnered, such as the Computer Security Institute sponsored by the Federal Bureau of Investigation. In the private sector numerous experts (e.g., scholars), professional organizations (e.g., American Bar Association and the American Institute of Certified Public Accountants), magazines (e.g., *Forbes, Seventeen*), and other groups are active in surveying their readers or members.

The Uniform Crime Reports (UCR), the dominant government collection repository for crime statistics in the United States, has noticeable flaws. Among the numerous criticisms directed at the UCR is that it fails to do a good job of including all kinds of crime. This problem is magnified with cybercrime. According to one expert, "The relatively hidden nature of the Internet crimes may lead to them going unnoticed. Unfamiliarity with laws covering computer-related crimes may lead victims to be unaware that a particular activity is in fact illegal."[3]

Although there are periodic statistical studies of specific types of cybercrimes, a full accounting of cybercrimes is almost next to impossible. In short, cybercrimes may go undetected and unreported or underreported.

On the other hand, victimization surveys that ask individuals and organizations whether they have experienced cybercrime are somewhat more reliable in accounting for cybercrimes. Most targets of cybercrime are reluctant to report these illegal acts to the authorities, but may feel more comfortable doing it in the context of an anonymous survey. According to McQuade, "What we know from research comes primarily from a very limited number of self-report offender or victimization studies conducted sporadically since the early 1990s."[4]

This has not stopped government entities and news reporters from trying to gather information about cybercrime. For example, the American-based National White-Collar Crime Center and the National Fraud Information Center have periodically administered victimization surveys to businesses. In 2000 the Bureau of Justice Statistics, which is part of U.S. Department of Justice, started the Cybercrime Statistics Program to "measure changes in the incidence, magnitude, and consequences of electronic crime."[5] Likewise, both the front and business pages of daily newspapers, as well as magazines devoted to computer users, routinely run stories on cybercrimes.

One of the most frequently cited sources of data is the Federal Bureau of Investigation's (FBI) Computer Security Institute. This organization produces the results of an annual computer security survey that asks U.S. corporations, government agencies, financial institutions, medical institutions, and universities about their victimization. Additional sources of data are the U.S. National Criminal Victimization Survey and the British Crime Survey. These are administered to households in their respective countries. Each time these data collection instruments are given, more questions are inserted to determine the broad range of victimization by cybercrimes.

In 2001, the U.S. Department of Justice's Bureau of Justice Statistics (BJS), in conjunction with the U.S. Census Bureau, conducted the very first federal government pilot victimization study of cybercrime. The report, released four years later, concluded that 42 percent of the businesses surveyed experienced some form of victimization. The majority of reported crimes were viruses, denial of service attacks, vandalism to a Web site, and damage to internal systems data. On a lesser scale, the firms said that they had been subject to embezzlement scams, fraud, and theft of corporate secrets.

Likewise, a handful of prominent consulting firms conduct similar studies of cybercrimes. Their research suggests that, on an individual level, cybercrimes may not be serious, but when the number of people, organizations, and businesses that are victimized on a global basis are added up, the numbers appear to be staggering. Moreover, some experts have suggested that cybercrime will become an increasingly large percentage of all crime in the twenty-first century.

Most commentators have decried the problem with statistics, and suggest that private industry collects this data in order to convince potential customers about the seriousness of the cybercrime threat to attract more business. Moreover, there is little consistency and rigorousness in how these private industry studies are conducted. Nevertheless, if these findings are cautiously interpreted, they can provide an idea of the seriousness of cybercrime.[6]

There are numerous reasons for underreporting cybercrime. These actions sometimes may be reported to a financial institution, but for a variety of reasons, the bank, brokerage house, or mutual fund does not pass on the information to law enforcement agencies. Alternatively, victims may not know they have been defrauded or victimized. They may not notice that money has been taken out of a bank or stock brokerage account or may see it as some sort of miscellaneous bank charge. Then again, the financial institution may not want to report the crime to either law enforcement or the client for fear that consumer confidence in the company will erode.

THE STUDY OF CYBERCRIME

The study of cybercrime as an academic field is in its infancy. Few colleges and universities have stand-alone classes in the subject. Cybercrime also depends on concepts, ideas, and methodology from other fields. The study of cybercrime takes into account that criminology and criminal justice are multi- and interdisciplinary fields. They draw on many different subjects such as engineering and the hard sciences, including, physics, computer science, and others. No longer confined to the fields of criminology, criminal justice, and computer sciences, scholars from such diverse subjects as cultural and media studies and business have contributed to knowledge about cybercrime.

Another issue is that compared to traditional crimes, such as street crime, there is not a lot of research being done in the field of cybercrime. This is due to a lack of well-trained scholars, the high cost of doing research in this area, lack of accurate data, and the constantly evolving nature of cybercrime.

Nevertheless, one indication of the growing study of cybercrime is the creation of an online academic journal called the *International Journal of Cyber Criminology*. In addition, while a handful of popular books on the topic are available, major textbook publishers have recently released books about the field of cybercrime. Likewise, a handful of scholarly and university presses have released books on the subject.

One of the biggest problems with research and writing about cybercrime is that the books are often outdated by the time they're published. Moreover, it might be difficult to attract an author to write such a book because experts are in high demand for other, more lucrative activities. There also is considerable misinformation about cybercrimes, cybercriminals, and cyberattacks. Numerous stereotypes of computer criminals exist.

CYBERCRIME IN POPULAR CULTURE

Regardless of how much actual cybercrime occurs in society, it is important to recognize how the concept is making its way into popular culture. Stories in comic books, fictional books, movies, and television shows have all integrated aspects of cybercrime. A big part of the public awareness of cybercrime comes from Hollywood movies that have featured characters either committing or responding to crimes with the use of computers and the Internet. According to criminologist Michael Levi, cybercrime "is used as a titillating entertainment which generates fear at the power of technology beyond the control of respectable society."[7]

Wall divides the history of cybercrime in commercial films into three generations:

> The first are the early generation films defined by the "hack" into an infrastructural system—*Italian Job*, 1969; *Die Hard*,

1988. They were followed by a second generation of films that were defined by, and romanticized, the gender (male) "hacker"—*War Games*, 1983. The later second generation films shifted from portraying hackers across communication networks to hackers in different types of virtualized environments, with hackers still young, but less gender specific and less likely to adopt moral highgrounds as in earlier films— *Johnny Mnemonic*, 1995; *Independence Day*, 1996. The third generation of films were defined by both "hacker and hack" being in virtual environments and epitomized by *The Matrix*, 1999.[8]

Some of the most influential Hollywood movies incorporating cybercrimes are *War Games, Sneakers, Hackers, The Net, Live Free or Die Hard*, and *Untraceable*.

War Games (1983), starring Matthew Broderick and Ally Sheedy, depicts a young, brash student, who—after successfully hacking into the Seattle public school system computers— eventually hacks into the U.S. Department of Defense computer system. He subsequently manages to bring the United States to the brink of launching World War III with an attack against the Soviet Union. The movie begins with the North American Aerospace Defense Command (NORAD) decision to automate the nuclear missile launching capability of the United States. The character portrayed by Broderick mistakenly starts a computer program that indicates that the Soviet Union is mounting a military attack on the United States. Broderick is discovered and arrested by the FBI and taken to NORAD's Cheyenne Mountain headquarters in Colorado, where he escapes with Sheedy's help. He then partners with the original software developer in order to reverse the program that has placed the Soviet Union on a false collision course with the United States.

Sneakers (1992), starring Dan Ackroyd, Ben Kingsley, Sidney Poitier, River Phoenix, and Robert Redford, follows the exploits of corporate computer-security experts hired by an organization they are led to believe is the U.S. National Security Agency to obtain a "black box" capable of decoding encrypted messages. This is a complicated movie with numerous murders and deceits. The team later gets the real NSA involved, and the proper use of the black box is held in dispute.

Hackers (1995) stars Jonny Lee Miller and Angelina Jolie, who portray high school students Dade Miller and Kate Libby, respectively. Miller is living in Seattle and is arrested for helping to simultaneously crash close to 1,500 computers. He is banned from using a computer until he is 18, and moves with his mother to New York City. There Miller meets Libby and falls in with a crowd of hackers at his new high school. One of his buddies manages to get access to a corporation and downloads what he believes is a garbage computer file. It turns out that the file has information that reveals a corporate executive's plan to "salami slice" a considerable amount of money. As a result, a cat-and-mouse game ensues.

The Net (1995), starring Sandra Bullock, Jeremy Northam, and Dennis Miller, revolves around Bullock's character, Angela Bennett/ Ruth Marx, who is a computer programmer. After a coworker sends her a file with instructions to open it, she does so and realizes that it takes her to a Web site controlled by the U.S. military. Then, while on vacation in Mexico, she meets a so-called hacker who turns out to be a cyberterrorist. He threatens her in an attempt to steal the computer program, but she escapes, only to find out that a criminal gang has changed her identity to that of a known felon so she won't be able to re-enter the United States. She ends up sending a message to the FBI while at a cybercrime conference and ultimately defeats the bad guys.

Live Free or Die Hard (2007) is the fourth in a series of movies starring Bruce Willis as John McClane, a police officer. In this movie a disgruntled and out-of-work former government worker, Thomas Gabriel, successfully disrupts a series of vital computer networks connected to air traffic control systems and ground transportation control systems in cities. The nefarious mastermind's ultimate goal is a "fire sale"—a combined computer attack to take down the United States's financial, transportation, and utilities systems—unless he is paid a healthy ransom. Meanwhile, Willis's character arrests a computer hacker who helps him track Gabriel and fight his organization along the way. The bad guys take over the air traffic control system and crash a plane. In the end McClane gets his man.

Finally, the movie *Untraceable* (2008) stars Diane Lane as Jennifer March, an FBI agent who works in the cybercrime division. The plot involves a serial killer who broadcasts video of his victims via a Web site and sets up the site so that the more people who watch, the more quickly his victims approach death. March stumbles upon a Web site that initially broadcasts the poisoning death of animals, and then the site operator progresses to poisoning people. Naturally, March takes on the challenge of finding and capturing the killer.

These movies, most of which appear realistic, simultaneously exaggerate the threat of cybercrime, the ease with which semi-skilled individuals can operate undetected in committing these kinds of illegal actions, and the special skills and knowledge the fictional characters have. Most important, computer systems are a lot more difficult to hack than the directors of these movies let the audience believe.

THE CYBERCRIMINAL SUBCULTURE: THE PERPETRATORS

Cybercriminals, like other kinds of property offenders, have their own subculture (i.e., shared norms and/or ways of doing things). Learning how to commit cybercrime often takes place via conduits such as online chat rooms, magazines like *2600 Magazine* and *Phrack*, face-to-face communications, and—perhaps most importantly—trial-and-error experiences. Strange but true, there is an international conference called DEFCON that meets once a year in Las Vegas where hackers exchange their latest tricks.

The media often portrays cybercriminals with sensationalized and stereotypical descriptions. Most cybercriminals, however, exist in the shadows, not wishing to gain much exposure. Both the media and academics categorize cybercriminals so as to better predict and profile who is committing these kinds of crimes. However, as new types of cybercrime have emerged and been identified, classification has proven to be elusive. The reality is that many cybercriminals engage in many different kinds of crimes, making classification next to impossible and almost meaningless. Consequently, there is no widespread agreement about who cybercriminals are. If there were, it would be easier to compare them and to develop explanations and countermeasures to fight cybercrime.

Based on McQuade's research, the majority of cybercrimes are "inside jobs." They are committed by employees that have routine access to an organization's computers, and may also have some specialized knowledge in accounting, the law, or both.[9] According

A designer of consumer electronics hardware addresses the audience at DEFCON, an annual hacker conference held in Las Vegas, Nevada. *AP Photo/Jane Kalinowsky*

to De Angelis, "75 to 80 percent of prosecuted computer crimes are committed by current or former employees," not the malicious hackers common in popular culture.[10]

Then again, as McQuade points out, "Since the early days of known computer abuses, individuals who abuse and misuse computers have been stereotyped as being predominately young, educated, white males who are curious about computing and telecommunications technology, possess technical computer and programming skills, and have little if any criminal history."[11]

Organized cybercrime elements are also different from traditional organized crime groups. Current research indicates that cybercriminals will associate with other like-minded individuals for short periods of time, commit a crime or series of crimes, and then eventually disband. This doesn't mirror the "gang life" that exists in America's urban centers or the rackets of traditional organized crime run by groups such as the Mafia. It is also highly probable that, as cybercrime evolves, the various types of cybercriminals will increase.

Cybercriminals are likely to come from well-off segments of society. This may be because middle- or upper-class people have greater opportunities to use computers in their classrooms, businesses, and homes. In addition, these individuals typically have the financial resources to purchase the latest technology. People who attend poorer school districts, have unskilled jobs with minimal access to computers, or earn low wages have fewer opportunities to commit cybercrimes.

THE CAUSES OF CYBERCRIME

There are many popular explanations of why cybercrime takes place, but few scholars determine the causes using social science theories. Although there is no simple explanation why, theories help to explain the cybercrime phenomenon and help to specify ways authorities can minimize it or encourage certain types of actions to protect against it. McQuade, however, offers a particularly sophisticated theory of IT-enabled abuse and crime. He utilizes almost all available criminological theories. His theory of technology-enabled crime, policing, and security "incorporates many ideas expressed in earlier writings about the causes of crime combined with principles of technology invention, innovation, adoption, implementation, training, use, personnel supervision, maintenance, evaluation, and diffusion."[12] It suggests that there is an informal competition between criminals adopting new ways of criminal activity and law enforcement officials lagging behind in forming policies to respond. Meanwhile, the media disseminates information about the crimes and the public (and often private corporations) starts taking precautions that minimize the opportunities for victimization.

THE EFFECTS OF CYBERCRIME

There are numerous consequences of cybercrime that impact the public, students, law enforcement, and other individuals and groups. The most notable consequence is victimization, from data loss and theft of property or money to the considerable expense, time, and frustration often required to fix the problems caused by a cybercrime. The reactions depend on numerous factors, including the type and duration of victimization, which can be short or long term. Moreover, some types of software programs, Web sites, and attachments pose a greater risk for cybercrime than others. McQuade says, "Cybercrime victimization most often involves infected software, damaged hardware systems, and destruction, denial, degradation, or theft of data. This includes information pertaining to personal and professional contacts, schedules and travel plans, online purchases

♀ SYNONYMS FOR CYBERCRIME

- computer abuse
- computer crime
- computer fraud
- computer-related crime
- crime by keyboard
- cyber attack
- cyber theft
- electronic crime
- high-technology crime
- information technology crime
- Internet crime

and financial accounts data, health and medical records, academic grades and so on."[13]

The problem of cybercrime has led to the proliferation of computer security products as well as experts who will, for a fee, fix computers that are infected with all sorts of malware. These specialists also may consult with individuals, companies, and organizations and instruct them on the best ways to minimize the danger of cybercrime and fend off attacks. This is discussed further in Chapter 7.

Once targeted, it can take a long time for victims of identity theft to clear their name and repair their credit. This can lead to rejection of employment for certain types of jobs, denial of credit if the targeted individual wants to buy a home or car, and other financial problems.

Hacking
and Malware

On November 2, 1988, Robert Morris, who at the time was working on his graduate degree in computer science at Cornell University, wrote a computer program (later dubbed the Morris Worm), with which he intended to measure the size of the Internet. However, a mistake in the code made the program dangerous. Morris and others could not believe the kind of damage his program caused. Only intending to run on the computers in his lab, the program replicated itself with amazing speed and extended beyond Morris's workplace. The program led to computers shutting down. Businesses that owned the infected computers lost countless dollars due to inactivity or time spent trying to remedy the situation. When all was said and done, the worm infected between 2,000 and 3,000 computers. In 1989, Morris became one of the first people to be prosecuted under the relatively recent federal *Computer Fraud and Abuse Act*. After serving three-year's probation, he created a lucrative software company, sold it, and is now a professor at MIT.

Throughout history some workers upset with their bosses, supervisors, the business owners, or the government they worked for resorted to sabotage or vandalism. This often included damaging the machines they worked on or ruining the crops they were supposed to tend. Such actions are popularly called "monkey wrenching." Also, some young people engage in acts of vandalism as a protest against authorities and authority figures, such as parents, teachers, and law enforcement officers. This includes throwing rocks at windows, damaging school property, writing graffiti on walls, and so on. Vandalism, which is illegal, is often a malicious

Robert Morris leaves Federal Court in Syracuse, New York, in January 1990. He was found guilty of violating federal computer tampering laws in connection with a computer worm he created while a student at Cornell University. *AP Photo/Michael J. Okoniewski*

way of lashing out against rules that are perceived to be unfair or ridiculous.

With the advent of the computer, the Internet, and the Web, the opportunities for vandalism have increased. Every day unauthorized individuals manage to access restricted computer systems. They secure usernames and passwords for e-mail accounts or manage to log onto parts of a server that are meant to be unavailable to outsiders. Also, anyone with some basic computer programming skills can launch viruses, Trojan horses, worms, and other malware. These computer codes can upset if not destroy computer operating systems. These actions can be done remotely from anywhere in the world.

PHREAKING

Some of the earliest electronic thievery was committed by individuals known as **phreaks**. They exploited vulnerabilities in telephone systems to break into telephone voice mail and computer systems. Sometimes this was done simply to gain access to free long distance. One of the more notable exploits was the 1997 break-in to the New York City Police Department call center. Phreakers replaced the official message with one instructing callers that the police were too busy eating donuts and drinking coffee to respond to their calls. Over the last decade the reported incidence of phreaking has decreased and has been replaced by hackers and hacking.

HACKING

Hacking is the "unauthorized access and subsequent use of other people's computer systems."[1] Hacking can expose vulnerabilities in a computer system, but more importantly, it can also damage the system and integrity of the organization that owns it, particularly its ability to store sensitive information. Once the public learns that a company's computer system has been attacked, its customers may cease dealing with them, and others may avoid doing business with that company in the future.

Every year all sorts of organizations, such schools, businesses, and corporations, report more unauthorized intrusions into their computer systems. Once a hacker has access to a system he or she can steal computer resources, take proprietary or secret information, sabotage the system, or alter or destroy parts of the system. Other kinds of hacking crimes include "denial of service" (DOS) attacks, and sending malicious software.

Denial of service attacks, also known as a cyber-barrage or e-mail bombing, occur when there are large numbers of people (or more appropriately computers, as this process may be automated) trying to get access to a computer network or Web site by simultaneously logging in. This action often overloads the system, preventing access by legitimate users. This is similar to getting a constant busy signal when trying to call an airline during a snow emergency that is delaying flights. Denial of service can also be accomplished by trying to log into somebody's computer account with an incorrect password. In most systems, after a certain number of wrong entries, the account is locked and all further attempts are blocked for a period of time, thus frustrating the user from legitimately accessing the account. In 2000, for instance, the popular **search engine** Yahoo! was subjected to a DOS attack. Users who had Yahoo! e-mail accounts were prohibited from using them for approximately three hours.

When hacking first began it was done by people with minimal technical sophistication. By simply adding different extensions to Web site addresses, or uniform resource locators (URLs), it was often possible to get deeper into a corporation or organization's Web site. As preventive measures were taken by mainframe operators and computer programmers, this kind of access required sophisticated training and knowledge of software architecture. Nowadays there are many kinds of software available that makes hacking almost effortless. A random number generator password program can discover a protected password within a matter of minutes or hours, giving an individual or organization access to a bank account or computer program or system.

Although there are numerous hackers, few have the expert skills to penetrate sophisticated computer networks. Once an individual, team, or criminal organization has successfully hacked a computer they may engage in "data diddling." This is the manipulation, theft, or destruction of important data located on a computer, such as school grades, or business sales reports, payroll information, inventory, contracts, and contacts.

CAUSES OF HACKING

There are numerous explanations for why hackers engage in this kind of computer crime. Law enforcement and computer security professionals believe hackers are primarily motivated by maliciousness and a desire to destroy things, while hackers will claim that the primary reason for their unauthorized and illegal entering into computer systems is simply curiosity about them.[2]

A number of studies have interviewed hackers to determine why they commit or engage in their crimes. Also, hackers have written articles published on the Web or in print that explain their motivations. Many perpetrators have anarchist tendencies. They do not trust authority, especially concentrated governmental or corporate power. They portray themselves as modern-day Robin Hoods, stealing from the rich and distributing wealth to the poor. One of the most well-known credos is "The Conscience of a Hacker," also known as "The Hacker Manifesto." This statement (See box) outlines the utopian ethical basis for hackers' activities.

Insider accounts of what motivates hackers are at odds with the outsider explanations. The insiders stress a well-conceived (but morally questionable) rationale for why they engage in hacking. The so-called ethical hackers claim to be motivated "by factors such as intellectual curiosity, the desire to expand the boundaries of knowledge, a commitment to the free flow and exchange of information, resistance to political authoritarianism and corporate domination, and the aim of improving computer security by exposing the laxity and ineptitude of those charged with safeguarding socially sensitive data."[3] This is perhaps why there is a distinction between hackers, who are motivated by ethical reasons, and **crackers**, who

♀ THE HACKER MANIFESTO

In 1986 Loyd Blankenship, aka the Mentor, was arrested on suspicion of hacking into secured computer systems. Around that time Blankenship penned one of the most cited essays written by a hacker. The 450-word piece, "The Hacker Manifesto," was originally published in the underground **e-zine** *Phrack*. It stated: "Yes, I am a criminal. My crime is that of curiosity. My crime is that of judging people by what they say and think, not what they look like. My crime is that of outsmarting you, something that you will never forgive me for." In 1990, because of his continued involvement in the computer underground, Blankenship's home and employer were raided by the U.S. Secret Service. Apparently, the Secret Service was worried that a book Blankenship was writing would help others commit cybercrimes, although it was actually the rulebook for a new role-playing game. Blankenship currently works as a computer programmer and security researcher.

are motivated by malicious objectives. Obviously these are highly personal and subjective terms that hackers and crackers use among themselves.

Nevertheless, most hackers tend to be male adolescents and teenagers. Taylor suggests that "those who continued to hack into their mid-twenties complained that they were viewed as 'has-beens' by the youthful majority of the hacker underground."[4] Others go one step further and blame youth participation in hacking as a result of dysfunctional families. This theory has been criticized by many experts. For example, Wall identifies two basic types of hackers: white hats and black hats.[5] The white hats are motivated by intellectual curiosity and a need to demonstrate their problem-solving abilities. The black hats are mainly concerned with financial gain or revenge. The white hats are often considered to be ethical and the black hats unethical. Wall further divides white hats into three categories: gurus who are the experts, wizards who are known for their knowledge, and the Samurai, who hire themselves out to companies that want to test the vulnerabilities or the integrity of their computer systems. Samurai can also "hire themselves out to undertake legal 'cracking' tasks, legitimate or justified surveillance such as corporate disputes, assist lawyers working on privacy rights and First Amendment cases, and to assist any other parties that have legitimate reasons to need an electronic locksmith."[6]

On the other end of the spectrum, Wall categorizes unethical hackers into three groups, each with a different level of sophistication: utopians, cyberpunks, and script kiddies.[7] Utopians think that their activities are contributing to the betterment of society by demonstrating its weaknesses. Cyberpunks like to lash out at societal targets and damage them. The script kiddies are low-skilled individuals who use already written software to infiltrate computer systems.

One the mainstays of the hacker world is an e-zine called *Phrack*. This publication, which started in 1985, contains articles instructing readers how to gain unauthorized (and thus illegal) access into telephone lines (phreaking), ostensibly to place long distance phone calls without incurring charges. The magazine, now available online, provides advice on how to hack into computer systems. *Phrack* contained the now famous essay, "The Conscience of a Hacker," which glorified the hacker lifestyle.

SOCIAL ENGINEERING

One of the most common ways that hackers get access to computer accounts or computer systems is through a process called **social engineering**. This means using different ways to trick individuals into releasing critical information to a stranger. In general, this practice is simple. It often involves using flattery, deception, and intimidation to convince others to provide important information about their computer network. One of the earliest discussions of social engineering was written by Don Parker in his book *Crime by Computer* (1976). He identified various social engineering methods that cybercriminals use to elicit critical information out of individuals, ranging from name-dropping to frequently calling false alarms.

In 2002 Kevin Mitnick, a former self-confessed hacker who was convicted of several computer crimes, wrote the book, *The Art of Deception: Controlling the Human Element in Security*. It detailed how he skillfully, and without rousing the suspicion of those he talked to, managed to obtain critical information from people who work in information technology-related divisions of organizations. In general, he said, "The goal is to get people to do the bidding of the attackers, who often masquerade as someone in authority, someone in need, or someone with a rightful claim to specific information in order to accomplish a worthy task."[8] Mitnick further developed a five-part social engineering cycle, a conceptual scheme that is designed to elicit privileged information about computer security related matters. It involved:

1. identifying targets for deception
2. investigating them
3. establishing a rapport with them
4. upsetting the trust
5. using intelligence

HACKTIVISM

One relatively recent innovation has been the use of hacking that goes beyond sneaky thrills to use the Internet for political objectives. This is called "hacktivism." It can include such relatively innocuous and simple behaviors as creating or signing an online petition or it can be as damaging as cyberterrorism in which opponents to a political regime try to disrupt or disable computer

Computer hacker turned author Kevin Mitnick poses for a portrait in promotion of his book, *The Art of Deception: Controlling the Human Element in Security,* in June 2002. AP Photo/Joe Cavaretta

systems responsible for running a country's critical infrastructure. Although defining these practices is relatively easy, it is not always easy to distinguish between them. Hacktivism is the combination of hacking or computer communications with political activism. Cyberterrorism refers to "the exploitation of electronic vulnerabilities by terrorist groups in pursuit of their political aims."[9]

The Internet has allowed governments, political parties, and activist groups to store information and mobilize constituencies. There are numerous benefits of hacktivism. It is a way to connect like-minded individuals who are geographically spread out but united for or against a common issue they care about. It can also offer participants or signatories a measure of anonymity when signing online petitions. Also, information regarding where a protest meeting might take place and directions to get to the location can be distributed online.

The Internet is useful for both political activists and terrorists in communicating, coordinating, rapidly spreading messages, recruiting members, conducting research, and raising money for a cause. Over the past two decades there have been a handful of well-publicized cases of individuals and groups that have gained access to U.S. Department of Defense (DOD) computers. In 1986, for example, a group of West German teenagers, known as the Chaos Club, managed to access DOD systems. Apparently they were selling this information to the KGB, the intelligence agency in the Soviet Union.

Another kind of hacktivism is called "cyber defacement" or "Web defacement." This is when relatively sophisticated hackers get access to an inadequately protected Web site and then leave a message on one of the pages to show that they successfully hacked the site. Alternatively, they may place some sort of pornographic image or offensive statement on one of the pages. Religious and political Web sites are prone to these sorts of attacks.

Finally, thinking about starting a Web site that criticizes a business? Despite protests that one's free speech rights have been abrogated, creating such a site may also create a legal nightmare. People who use this strategy to complain online should be prepared for a cease and desist order from the targeted corporation's lawyer or law firm. They may claim trademark or copyright infringement or launch a defamation or libel lawsuit against the Web site and its creator. Even if one's claims are true, most well financed corporations don't like their reputations tarnished on the Web and will retaliate against those who make them look bad. Those considering an action like this are recommended to consult http://www.webgripesites.com.

DISTRIBUTION OF MALWARE: VIRUSES, TROJAN HORSES, WORMS, ADWARE, AND SPYWARE

Malware is the general term for malicious software programs, including viruses, Trojan horses, worms, spyware, and adware.

These programs negatively impact the operating systems of computers, causing them to slow down and sometimes crash. Malware typically attaches to computer files and data. They include registry changes so that users are automatically redirected to another Web site when they try to open the Web site of their choosing. Sometimes these sites are pornographic in nature. The presence of malware may force a computer user to spend hours on the telephone dealing with a computer tech working for the computer's manufacturer, or a software or antivirus company.

There is a perception that the frequency and severity of malware will increase because of the greater numbers of people who are using the Internet and the sophistication that malware writers have to launch attacks. Also, it is now easier to target software applications. "Reasons for these trends include the combination of rapidly expanding telecommunications and high speed Internet connectivity, increased computing power, user friendliness and technological interoperability of software systems and electronic devices, increased opportunities to commit IT-enabled abuse and crime as the number of computer networks. . . ."[10]

Recent developments in malware include a higher level of automation that can scan for victims with vulnerable computer systems, bypass virus protection and detection software, and disable firewalls. Many kinds of malware are preceded by legitimate looking messages appearing to come from virus protection software. These messages indicate that a system has been hit by a virus, worm, or Trojan horse, and give explicit instructions about what to do. Unfortunately, following this phony advice only opens the computer system up to more viruses.

Viruses. Over the past decade there has been a proliferation of individuals and groups capable of sending annoying and debilitating computer viruses that quickly spread through the Internet. A virus "reproduces itself without the user's knowledge or permission by searching out and embedding itself into executable programs."[11] One of the very first viruses known to computer users was the Pakistani Brain virus. In January 1986 two brothers from Lahore, Pakistan, who operated a medical software company, embedded what turned out to be a malicious code in some of the software that they were selling. The software was widely purchased and distributed. When the software, which was on a floppy

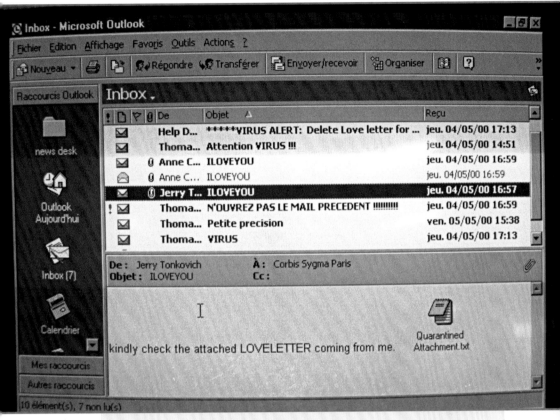

A computer screen displays an email inbox with several messages that contain the so-called ILOVEYOU computer virus. The virus was released in 2000 by Philippino computer student Onel De Guzman. *Serra Antoine/Corbis Sygma*

disk, loaded up it started deleting files in the targeted computers. The software came equipped, however, with information about the two individuals who created it, including their names and contact information, which led authorities to them. The brothers had created the virus as a way to fight pirates who illegally copied their software and had not intended to harm the computers of legitimate users.

In September 1998, the Chernobyl (also known as Spacefiller) virus was created. It "spread via users executing an infected file often attached to an email message. It was designed simply to erase the entire hard drive and overwrite the system BIOS [Basic Input/ Output System] of a victim's computer."[12]

In May 2000, Filipino computer student Onel De Guzman launched the ILOVEYOU virus. It worked by attaching itself to individual e-mails, and it was estimated to have caused $10 billion dollars in damages. Within days the FBI was able to determine the location and identity of the computer where the virus originated. Because of weak cybercrime laws in the Philippines, however, Guzman was left practically untouched by the episode.

In July 2001, the Red Code virus—which defaced Web sites and left the message "hacked by the Chinese"—had infected close to 250,000 computers, prompting fears by government officials that it could slow the Internet when it re-emerged on August 1. In 2003, the Sobig.F worm "stole addresses from victims' computers and spread so rapidly that nearly six percent of all Internet email traffic contained the worm."[13]

Often initiated for malicious motives, these viruses corrupt or delete software, operating systems, and other important files on a computer. They can also cause personal computers and mainframe systems to slow down or even come to a crashing halt. Public scares and panics about these kinds of crimes seem to be a daily event in our lives. Take for example the Y2K Millennium Bug scare. Computer users were worried that software programmers had not taken into consideration the fact that when the new millennium started, years would begin with "20" rather "19." Computer users were warned that when the year changed from 1999 to 2000, things taken for granted that were either partially or fully based on automated computer programs might cease to work or function properly. People expressed fears about being on an elevator, subway, or plane anytime around midnight on New Year's Eve. In fact, very few reported instances of computers malfunctioning occurred. This may have been because efforts to fix the problem were put into place in the years leading up to the change or because the Millennium problem simply was not a problem after all.

Viruses often target computers that use Microsoft's Internet Explorer, one of the most popular Web browsers on the market. Explorer and other Web browsers allow individuals to navigate the Web with a great degree of ease. Beginning in the late 1990s, computer users who used Explorer were at risk of receiving all kinds of malware threats. This prompted Microsoft and other software security companies (e.g., Norton and McAfee) to develop a series of patches that would prevent, minimize, or remedy computers from frequently being attacked. To avoid the problems associated with Explorer, many users switched to the Firefox search engine produced by the Mozilla Foundation (http://www.mozilla.org) or the Safari search engine produced by the Apple Corporation (http://www.apple.com).

Trojan horses. Trojan horses are computer software or code that a user thinks is supposed to be performing a beneficial action, but instead it does something else that is harmful to the computer. Its name comes from the classic Greek mythology story in which the citizens of Troy are given what appears to be a large, wooden horse by their enemies, the Greeks. They take the horse inside their city gates, but it only leads to their defeat when soldiers hiding inside the horse descend and attack the citizens at night. Trojan horses can be in the form of free screen savers or programs designed to detect and repair malware. They can allow remote access to a computer by unauthorized users, which ends up destroying programs on the computer.

Worms. Worms are computer programs that reproduce themselves. Unlike viruses they do not need to attach themselves to programs. Worms, "do not need to be clicked on and executed to carry out any number of functions ranging from annoying to destructive."[14] Their major damaging effect is eating up bandwidth, or memory, on a hard drive. Worms are often sent via spam and are activated when a user opens the e-mail from the spam message. This is similar to opening your front door to strangers. Numerous worms are released on the Internet each day. One of the first worms was identified during the 1970s, and their numbers have increased since then. Over the past decade four notable worms have done the most amount of damage: the Morris Worm, WANK Worm, Blaster Worm, and the My Doom Worm.

In November 1988, Robert Morris Jr., a student at Cornell University and the son of the chief scientist for the U.S. National Computer Security Center, released one of the very first Internet worms. Machines infected by the worm slowed down until they no longer worked.

In 1989, antinuclear hackers, whose identities have never been confirmed, launched the WANK Worm. WANK, the acronym for Worms Against Nuclear Killers, only affected computers made by the now-defunct Digital Equipment Corporation (DEC). It was sent to protest a National Aeronautics and Space Administration (NASA) space probe that had nuclear materials. The worm "was claimed to have cost NASA up to half a million dollars, but failed to prevent the probe's launch."[15]

In August 2003, 18-year-old American Jeffrey Parson launched Variant B of the Blaster Worm. "This computer virus infected nearly 50,000 computers, caused millions of dollars in damage, and shook confidence in the trustworthiness of the Internet. At sentencing [the judge said that Parson] had been a loner who spent long periods of time holed up in his house using his computer, with virtually no human interaction, much less parental supervision."[16] In 2005, Parson was sentenced to 18 months in federal prison.

Spyware. Spyware is software or a computer code that is surreptitiously installed on a person's computer. Spyware has the ability to record an individual's keystrokes (e.g., keylogger), the Web sites he or she visits, and settings the user has selected (e.g., homepages). It can prevent the user from visiting certain Web pages or steal his or her passwords. Spyware also slows down a computer's browsing ability.

Adware. A variant of spyware is adware. This kind of software notes what kinds of sites a person visits. Adware helps marketers target their spam and provides them with market research information. Adware is picked up by computers when users visit Web sites that track their usage. It can slow down users' Internet surfing or browsing. Most computer security programs have adware-blocking capability.

Logic bombs. Another kind of malware is called a logic bomb. This occurs when a hacker gets access to a computer system and leaves some sort of malicious code capable of destroying or disabling parts or all of the system at a later time. Logic bombs are sometimes installed by disgruntled workers. The idea is that the action will take place in the future if the culprit is not paid some sort of ransom. The logic bomb is a variation of a virus.

One of the most well-known logic bombs was the Michelangelo virus, which was programmed to activate on March 6, 1992. Once activated, the virus had the ability to shut down a computer. The machine would not turn on, and any data on the computer was overwritten. Although it was first discovered in April 1991, many companies were caught off guard. Newspaper reports published around this time indicate that the virus infected approximately 10,000 computers.[17]

MOTIVATIONS OF CRACKERS, HACKERS, AND VIRUS OR WORM WRITERS

Because of the tendency for cybercrime to go unreported to authorities, knowledge about its perpetrators is limited. Much more is known about the victims than the perpetrators who lurk in the netherworld of the Internet. Nevertheless some information about why hackers do what they do is known. Wall identifies seven major motivations:

1. self-satisfaction
2. wanting respect from peers
3. currying favor with possible employers
4. illegal financial gain
5. revenge
6. distance from victim
7. political protest.[18]

According to Wall, hackers "tend to be more reserved, often revelling in distancing themselves from their victims and shunning contact. . . .there survive many chat groups devoted to brokering information about offending activities."[19] Wall further notes that "traditional, skilled, and hacking, or cracking, has morphed into something quite different, presenting a range of new threats and exposing network users to a range of new risks."[20] It is also understood that many of the hackers learn their skills online through chat rooms and other similar forums.

♀ INFAMOUS CYBERCRIMINALS

The 414s (American): This gang of teenagers broke into computers of Los Alamos National Laboratory, Sloan-Kettering Cancer Center, and Security Pacific Bank, during the 1980s.

Abene, Mark (American): In the 1990s, along with co-conspirators from his gang known as the Masters of Deception, Abene hacked into several computer and telephone systems. He was investigated in connection with numerous intrusions into corporate systems and spent one year behind bars in a federal prison for his actions.

Botby, Adam (American): In 2003, along with accomplice Brian Salcedeo, Botby hacked into the Lowes retailer computer system.

Even-Chaim, Nahshon (Australian): During the 1980s, Even-Chaim hacked into computer systems of defense and nuclear research and weapons manufacturers in Australia and the United States.

Johansen, Jon Lech (Norwegian): Johansen wrote DeCSSS, a descrambling program that enabled individuals to watch pirated DVDs on their home computers. He was prosecuted in 2002 by Norwegian courts at the insistence of the Motion Picture Association of America, but he was not convicted of any crime. Since that time he has been developing reverse engineer deencryption software for different applications.

Lamo, Adrian (American): Known as "the homeless hacker," Lamo broke into the computers at the *New York Times*, Microsoft, Yahoo!, Bank of America, Citigroup, and Cingular in 2002.

McKinnon, Gary (British): Also known as "Solo," McKinnon was accused of hacking into 97 U.S. military and NASA computers in 2001 and 2002.

Mitnick, Kevin (American): One of the most well-known hackers, Mitnick was sentenced in 1999 to 46 months in federal prison for hacking into computer systems and stealing proprietary software. He is the author (with W.A. Simon) of two popular books: *The Art of Deception* and *The Art of Intrusion*.

Morris, Robert Tappan (American): Morris created and released the Morris Worm in 1988.

CYBERTERRORISM

There are several definitions of terrorism, but one of the most important was developed by well-respected terrorism expert Alex Schmid. He stated:

> Terrorism is a method of combat in which random or symbolic victims serve as . . . *target[s] of violence.* . . . Through [the] previous use of violence or the credible threat of violence other members of that group . . . are put in a *state of chronic fear (terror).* . . . The victimization of the target . . . is considered extranormal by most observers . . . [which in turn] creates an . . . audience beyond the target of terror. . . . The purpose of [terrorism] . . . is either to immobilize the target of terror in order to produce disorientation and/or compliance, or to mobilize secondary *targets of demands* (e.g., a government) or *targets of attention* (e.g., public opinion).[21]

Although Schmid's definition is long and has been modified by others,[22] it is preferable over other definitions that are too ambiguous to identify acts of terrorism. Having a definition of terrorism minimizes the tendency to describe all acts of maliciousness on the computer, and in other media, as terrorism. There is considerable fear that terrorists will hack into the computer mainframes of critical U.S. infrastructures serving transportation, banks, the military, and other areas. Terrorists could then disrupt the computers and cause these industries and organizations to either slowdown, make mistakes, or come to a grinding halt.

The threat of cyberterrorism should also be seen in the context of the mythmaking connected to the Internet. Numerous stories describe how powerful the Internet is and how with a few keystrokes someone or some group with an ideological, political, or religious objective can disable critical computer information systems and cause unprecedented destruction and mayhem. Most of these pronouncements have been exaggerated. On the one hand, programming software architects have predicted these sorts of threats. Thus, they have created backup systems to protect computer systems from the threats. On the other hand, the scares have typically been advanced by security professionals and wannabees, individuals and organizations that make their income by protecting computer systems or would like to do so. More skeptical

⚲ WELL-KNOWN VIRUSES AND WORMS

- Code Red (2001)
- Creep (1971)
- Melissa (1999)
- Morris (1988)
- Pakistani virus/Pakistani brain virus (1986)
- Wabbit (1974)

commentators, however, claim there is little empirical evidence to "warrant the level of concern currently being generated over cyberterrorism, nor to justify the sweeping enhancement of state powers that are being instituted in order to respond to the supposed threat."[23]

Although attacks committed by terrorist groups have never been confirmed in the United States, American computer systems have experienced attacks by foreign governments.

It is claimed that two viruses, the Code Red DoS and the Nimda, launched in 2001, were developed by terrorists in order to test the vulnerability of U.S. cyber defenses.

In another case, named Moonlight Maze, investigators established that attacks on the Department of Defense computer systems in 1998 increased as cyber defenses were raised. It was also determined that attackers, traced back to a mainframe in the former Soviet Union, were monitoring U.S. military troop movements. In connection with these attacks, it was further concluded that several suspected Al Qaeda operatives have sophisticated computer science technical backgrounds. Some have experience in infrastructure control systems, and they have used computers outside the United States to conduct reconnaissance on national critical infrastructure defense capabilities.

In March and April of 2000, Vitek Boden, an Australian who was denied a job at Maroochy Sire (a sewage control system) launched 46 cyberattacks at the company. While not terrorism per se, these attacks led to the spillage of tons of raw sewage into the surrounding environment. The damage was significant. It caused the death of marine life, darkened waterways, and created an incredible smell.

Cyber Theft
and Illegal Goods

During a casual conversation with one of my classes of college students, I told them about a recently released movie I saw at a theater over the weekend. The subject moved toward my students' movie watching behavior. I asked them how many went out to see a movie last weekend. I discovered that very few indulged in this pastime. I assumed that this must be because of the costs of going out. I then asked how many subscribed to http://www.blockbuster.com or http://www.netflix.com, which offer inexpensive rentals. Once again they met me with blank stares. It was only after a few more minutes of probing questions that a handful broke down and told me that there was absolutely no need for them to leave the comfort of their homes or subscribe to a rental service as they could simply download new releases for free, from their computer, by accessing Web sites located offshore (in countries with weak copyright protection laws).

A considerable amount of computer crime targets unsuspecting computer users, including individuals, organizations, and businesses, with the intention of deceiving and ultimately defrauding them. These actions often involve illegally obtaining proprietary and private personal information such as customers' credit card numbers, Social Security numbers, usernames, passwords, and trade secrets of businesses and corporations. This type of crime can create enormous trouble in the form of compromised privacy and security for individuals who have their health and financial records located on these systems. In these situations a hacker who accesses someone else's bank account or credit card information can spend that person's money or pass the information on to someone who can. This is called cyber theft.

THEFT OF FINANCIAL INFORMATION

Most online businesses depend upon payment by credit card, debit card, or bank transfer. In fact, had the credit card not been invented during the 1960s the advent of e-commerce might have been delayed.

Many people are reluctant to use their credit cards over the World Wide Web, and for good reason: There are individuals and groups who use relatively sophisticated software to collect not only credit card and debit card numbers, but also usernames, passwords, and other kinds of financial identification people provide when making online purchases. This information is then used by criminals to buy goods and services or it is sold to others who will do the same. There are now gangs in countries all around the world that mine this information and use unsuspecting individuals' financial information to purchase items and services.

Criminals using this technique can either steal credit card numbers online or manufacture false credit card numbers using their victims' personal information; any purchases are then delivered to a location that the perpetrator knows to be safe. Subsequently, victims often end up paying for the charges because they either didn't notice the purchases or were unable to remove the illegal charges from their account.

The frequency and seriousness of credit card fraud has prompted many credit card companies to expand their fraud-detection capabilities and to require customers to provide their ZIP code or the three-digit security code on the back of credit and debit cards when making purchases. This additional information provides one more piece of secure data to the financial institution to ensure it is the card owner who is using the card rather than a thief.

Credit card companies are also paying much more attention to instances of unusual card activity. For example, imagine someone goes on an international trip. No sooner does that person make his or her first credit card purchase than the foreign transaction is noted by the credit card company, which may contact the customer to determine if it indeed is a legitimate sale. Why the extra caution?

The company clearly does not want to be held liable for fraudulent purchases.

PIRACY

When an author writes a book, a musician records an album, or a production company releases a new film, there is a reasonable expectation that they will earn money through the sale of these creative works. To ensure this, artists and businesses generally copyright their creative works or intellectual property by filing paperwork with a national body such as the U.S. Copyright Office (http://www.copyright.gov). Copyright laws ensure that if a substantial portion of a creative work is used by another party without permission, the copyright owner can take legal action to be fairly compensated. Copyright protections, however, are frequently violated because it is often easy to illegally reproduce another's work without permission.

Copying books. Thanks to the invention of the Xerox photocopier in the 1960s, individuals who want a copy of a book or other printed material, such as newspapers and magazines, are able to make a copy at will. The cost–benefit problem for those considering photocopying a book, however, is that the price, time, and effort of photocopying each individual page makes the value of doing so questionable; purchasing the actual book is often a cheaper, more sensible option. However, that is not the case with many textbooks and academic books, because the high price of those books generally exceeds the cost of photocopying the needed material. Meanwhile, corporations like Google have developed utility programs such as Google Book Search (http://www.google.com/books) that make it possible to read excerpts and entire books online. Students and researchers wanting to avoid the inconvenience of either purchasing a book or checking it out of a library often consult this source when gathering information.

Music piracy. The problem of music piracy is not new. During the 1960s and 1970s people could sneak recording devices into a concert or other music venue, such as a nightclub, to record live performances. Others might copy the music from a CD or record to a cassette tape and ignore the deteriorated sound quality. These

Jammie Thomas leaves the federal courthouse building in Duluth, Minnesota, in October 2007 with her attorney. Thomas was the first person to go to trial for alleged music pirating through illegal sharing of music files. *AP Photo/Julia Cheng*

practices are called "bootlegging." When CD burners became commonplace in the late 1990s, it prompted an underground demand for bootlegs. Modern technology and electronic gadgets in every shape and size have now made it even simpler for individuals and businesses to copy music from records, tapes, CDs, iPods, and the Internet without sacrificing much quality.

Although originally conceived in the late 1970s, the MP3 file format for digitalizing music was not fully engineered and sold to the public until the early 1990s. MP3 technology opened up a new mechanism for audio recording beyond CDs and allowed music to be shared and downloaded from or between computers. In 1999, Shawn Fanning, a teenager from Brockton, Massachusetts, developed a computer program called Napster that could be downloaded from the Internet for free. This program permitted its subscribers to surf the Napster site for other users who had songs they wanted and to then download that music to their computers for free. This process, called "file sharing," violated the copyrights owned by the musicians and their recording companies. The Recording Industry Association of America (RIAA) claimed that Napster was preventing their member artists from earning a phenomenal amount of revenue. As the result of a civil suit, Napster changed its business model and began to sell "soundtracks and CDs via direct sales and music downloading services for fees from which copyright allowances are paid."[1] However, the change has not stopped many users from using other kinds of software to illegally download and copy music.

This is why the Recording Industry Association of America and the British Phonographic Industry (organizations established to protect the rights of music industry professionals) have targeted perpetrators through lawsuits and advertising against this kind of pirating. According to Wall, "Perhaps uniquely, the 16,000 or more cases were mostly brought against individuals, but few have actually gone to court, with the majority being settled privately."[2] In a similar fashion, the Motion Picture Association of America (MPAA) has tried to sue individuals who own illegally copied DVDs of motion pictures.

Copying DVDs. Walk around the downtown streets of any big city and it is often possible to find newly released Hollywood movies for sale in DVD format. Take, for example, New York

City, where it is not uncommon for street vendors or even some stores to sell the latest DVDs or theatrical releases. They typically ask about $5 per movie, but sometimes will take as little as

A man arranges his stack of pirated DVDs on a sidewalk in Beijing in January 2005. Such examples of DVD piracy are common in cities around the world. *AP Photo*

$3. All told, this price is anywhere from one-third to one-half the price of what it would cost to see the movie at a regular theater.

Unfortunately, the reproduction quality on these DVDs is often quite poor. Some DVDs are downloaded from the Internet through a number of foreign Web sites that enable this kind of illegal activity. Others are recorded on one or more digital video cameras in a theatre and are then edited together later. The image may jiggle, numbers used for preproduction editing may appear on the side or bottom of the screen, or the movie may be shown from an awkward angle. It may be tempting to tolerate these inconveniences to reduce the cost of seeing new movies, but this also means that the actors, screenwriters, directors, and production companies that made the original movie will not receive the payment to which they are entitled for their efforts.

There are also Web sites where users can download current and old movies. With a high-speed Internet connection it may take an hour or as little as half an hour to do this. Nevertheless, simply because the movies can be downloaded for free does not mean doing so is legal. These downloads also deprive actors, screenwriters, and moviemaking companies from the royalties they are legitimately due.

One of the largest attempts to convict an individual suspected of DVD piracy focused on Norwegian computer guru Jon Lech Johansen. During the 1990s, Johansen developed a device that allowed users to descramble a code that prevented DVDs from being copied. He was charged with computer hacking, but was found not guilty. "The failure to convict Johansen did not prevent the MPAA from continuing to protect its interests. Since 2004, legal actions have been brought against file sharers, particularly the film indexing sites and television download sites. . . . The latter action was significant because of the increased use of the Internet as the broadcasting medium for television and the blurring of the boundaries between the two 'as TV-quality video on-line becomes a norm'."[3]

Copying software. Some—but not all—computer software is proprietary, and thus unauthorized copying and distribution is a form of digital piracy. Warez is the term used to describe illegally copied software. People who do the copying and distribution are known as pirates. Warez comes from the word wares. Software manufacturers originally provided little or no protection against copying, and it wasn't hard for people to figure out that it was as simple as copying one or two computer disks to run, for example, a word processing or statistical analysis program. This practice is called traditional pirating. Early software programs were very basic; they did not contain as many lines of code as software does today, and they were sometimes limited to a single floppy disk. Also, they often had no programmed protection against installing them on more than one computer. The early forms of warez included individuals who shared their computer software among family, friends, and acquaintances. People may not have considered that doing this was immoral, unethical, or illegal. The sharers, however, were in violation of state and federal copyright laws.

Over time, the ability and frequency of sharing computer files and software increased through the use of "file transfer protocol (FTP), USENET newsgroups, bulletin board systems (**BBS**), and Internet relay chat (IRC)."[4] Here, all one needs to do is log on to a Web site and download the desired program to a computer. Today there is a considerable amount of publicly legal software available on the Web that is supported by the Free Software Foundation (http://www.fsf.org).

One of the most well-known cases of illegal software copying involved American David LaMacchia, a student at the Massachusetts Institute of Technology. In 1994, he made software available through a BBS. Shortly thereafter LaMacchia was arrested by the FBI and charged with attempting to commit wire fraud. Because LaMacchia never profited from the action (the software he copied and offered was available for free) he was acquitted of all charges. Software manufacturers have complained for years that free, illegal software is common in many lesser-developed countries, where authorities are lax in enforcing copyright laws. In the United States this kind of illegal activity is monitored by the Software Manufacturers Association.

Illegal wireless access. A computer equipped with a **wireless** Internet card will typically try to find any connection that is in range. Users may be tempted to log on to the closest system. However, without permission from the network administrator, it is fraudulent to do so and is considered stealing someone else's signal. Doing so requires very little technical skill. Most wireless security systems recommend that users set up an encryption protocol on

A laptop computer screen displays a page from the file-sharing Web site thepiratebay.org. The four men behind the popular site went on trial in Stockholm, Sweden, in February 2009, accused of helping millions of users worldwide to break copyright laws. They were found guilty in April 2009 and sentenced to serve one year in prison and pay a fine of approximately $3.5 million. David Brabyn/Corbis

their modem that will prevent unauthorized users from accessing their wireless account. Users who choose not to do this might notice that their wireless network often runs slow and that they're regularly kicked off the system. This may happen because someone is pirating a signal. While there are many possible explanations for slowness, one of the most common is that someone nearby is piggybacking on a paid customer's wireless-enabled network.

COPYRIGHT INFRINGEMENT EXPANDED

Complicated laws, or copyrights, exist to protect the creative products of artists, authors, musicians, publishers, and others. According

to the International Intellectual Property Alliance, a group repre-
senting trade associations that have a vested interest in protecting copyrights, the theft of "U.S. copyrighted materials results in
$20–22 billion in losses to rights-holders excluding growing levels
of piracy via the Internet."[5] Piracy is abundant. It is committed by
people from all income levels and all ages who don't consider themselves criminals or don't think they're committing illegal activities.
As a result, there have been national and international efforts to
curtail this kind of activity.

Some in the music industry have made a counterargument
against rigid copyright enforcement, claiming that illegally copied
music has, in fact, led to growth in music sales. This perspective
is based on the belief that, once an individual has the music file—
however it is obtained—he or she is more inclined to legally purchase a CD from that same artist or to go to a live performance.
Thus, there is "a rising tide saves all ships" effect. This phenomenon has been echoed "by the commercial success of recently
introduced, and authorized pay-to-use MP3 sites, such as iTunes,
e-Music and others, and, of course, the popularity of new MP3 play-
ing hardware devices, such as the iPod. Further evidence of this
trend is found in empirical research conducted in 2005 by Leading
Question, which found that online file sharers actually buy more
music, up to four-and-a-half times more, in legal downloads."[6]

ONLINE FRAUD

The World Wide Web has opened multiple opportunities for individuals and organizations to defraud consumers and the general public
of their hard earned income and savings. These include scams that
involve selling false goods or services and with failing to ship the
goods customers have purchased.

Selling false goods online. One of the biggest scares today
involves fraudulent acts committed through online auction sites
such as eBay. Although eBay and other sites have cracked down on
scams, consumers still get burned. These sites can produce numerous opportunities for fraud: The goods offered for sale may be stolen
or counterfeit, purchased items may not be delivered, or the actual
products may not be what were promised. Alternatively, there are
a number of scams being run through http://www.craigslist.com, a

💡 SAMPLE RESPONSE OF SOMEONE WITH BAD INTENTIONS

Scammers try to trick people out of goods by sending a bad check and then picking up the item or items before the seller realizes they're being ripped off. Notice the misspelled words and overly accommodating tone that is often found in scam communications.

Hello,

Thanks for the prompt response. I will love I just checked ur profile and i liked it so i thought i should reply. . . Actually, I got your words and it really impressed me so much, well to make an instant purchase, so please do withdraw the advert from Craigslist, i don't mind adding an extra $50 dolls for you to do that so that i can be rest assured that the item is in hand. I will also like you to know that I will be paying via check, and it will be over night payment due to the distance. I am currently in the Uk and i am Relocating down to the US to do a survey for my employer (GMC Insurance Group (UK), as we are about to open an office in the state. You don't need to bother your self with the shipment. Ok? My interior decorator who will be handling the renting of an appartment, purchase of entertainment system and other appliances that i will need in the USA will take care of that. He will as well be incharge of moving down my luggages down to the states.. So i will need you to provide me with the following information to facilitate the mailing of the check.

Name:............
Address:.............
Phone number(cell and land):............

 Once again ,I will like you to know that you will not be responsible for shipping I will have my interior decorator come over as soon as you have cashed the check
Have a nice day.
John

Web site that allows users to post items for sale without incurring a charge. Here, sellers can fall victim to individuals who ask to have the items shipped to them out of town with the promise that they'll mail a check or deposit the agreed-upon sum into the seller's bank account. The buyer might even promise to send a truck to pick up the items. The vehicle comes to pick up the merchandise, but the seller never gets the money. In short, the thief picks up the goods before the seller finds out that the check is inauthentic or bounces (does not clear because of insufficient funds).

Nigerian/Spanish prisoner fraud. Many other computer- or Web-based schemes exist, including the Nigerian or Spanish prisoner fraud. In this case, someone contacts the victim via the Internet and claims to be an expatriate or close relative of an exiled, deposed, or deceased member of a foreign government. This person says he or she has considerable sums tied up in a bank or safety deposit bank that temporarily cannot be accessed. He or she then tries to appeal to the victim's good moral character and suggests that the victim has been contacted because of his or her trustworthiness. The scammer also offers to share his or her wealth with the victim in exchange for the help; the catch is that the victim must first put up some of his or her own money to cover bank fees or taxes so the money can be accessed. Despite the scammer's promises of legitimacy, individuals who fall victim to this type of deceit and send money aren't likely to ever recover those funds. Similar types of scams are done with messages stating that the victim is the recipient of lottery funds.

OTHER KINDS OF CYBER THEFT

One of the more novel ways in which cybercriminals have engaged in computer crimes has been through the acquisition of improperly discarded computers. This equipment tends to contain a treasure trove of "sensitive/confidential information [including] deleted files, recovery partitions, configuration files, password storage and special hardware devices."[7] One such instance occurred in 2002, "when the U.S. Veterans' Administration Medical Center in Indianapolis discarded 140 desktop computers, many of which were sold on the open market. It was later discovered that several of these computers' hard drives contained sensitive medical and financial

⚲ MAJOR CYBERCRIMES

In May 2001, FBI investigators filed charges for credit card fraud, bank fraud, and other online fraud totaling an estimated $117 million against almost 100 individuals and businesses as part of Operation CyberLoss. In March 2001, Bibliofind.com, a book vendor, revealed that its servers, holding customers' credit card data, had been subjected to a security breach that lasted four months.

information, including the active government credit card numbers and information identifying patients diagnosed with AIDS and mental health problems."[8]

Most people believe that by deleting their computer files they are removing all compromising or sensitive information. The truth is that software manufacturers have developed their systems to visibly remove the files for the average user and allow memory space to be used for other purposes. Their content, however, is actually still present in secluded portions of the hard drive for later retrieval by experts. According to experts like Dale L. Lundsford and Walter A. Robbins, computer criminals look for data "in five areas of computers: deleted files, recovery partitions, configuration files, password storage, and special hardware devices."[9] In order to protect organizations and companies from this kind of crime, computer security experts recommend that these computers be sanitized using computer programs designed to delete all hidden files.

USING THE INTERNET TO SELL ILLEGAL GOODS

Using the Internet to distribute information about committing a crime, such as how to manufacture illegal drugs like LSD or speed; the sale, manufacture, or conversion of illegal weapons; and the sale or construction of explosive devices, bombs, or trade in endangered species wildlife is illegal. Here one must be careful about distinguishing between thoughts and deeds.

Both legal and illegal drugs are available on the Internet. They may be sold by legal or illegal entities. Dangers arise when prescription drugs are sold to minors or people who have no pre-scription for them. Many of these drugs are shipped from outside the country, thereby passing quality control protocols established here in the United States and United States Postal Service security procedures. These drugs may be ineffective or even deadly if their contents are not what the purchaser is expecting.

Identity Theft and Phishing

In June 2008 Patrick Kalonji was arrested in Massachusetts in connection with running the largest identity theft ring in the United States. In August 2008, through a joint operation of the Department of Justice with counterparts in Turkey and Germany, his accomplices were also taken into custody. He allegedly had stolen the identities of 150 people from online gambling Web sites and passed this information on to his gang. According to then Attorney General Michael B. Mukasey, "We have charged a total of 11 people, including residents of at least five different countries, with various crimes relating to the theft and resale of credit and debit card account information." Apparently they used "sophisticated computer hacking techniques, breaching security systems and installing programs that gathered enormous quantities of personal financial data," Mukasey added.

Among computer owners and users, the Web has become one of the first places most people consult for information and thus it is a valuable conduit to collect information about both people and organizations. The Web can also be used to lure individuals to sites where this data is collected. This kind of surreptitious information collection is crucial to cybercriminals who engage in identity theft. Because there is big money at stake and the financial rewards for criminals are almost limitless, they go to amazing lengths to defraud their victims.

IDENTITY THEFT

One of the recurrent problems with the Web is how criminals use stolen personal information to pretend they are someone else, open credit cards in that person's name, and run up big bills that then go to that person. This crime isn't new to the Internet and has existed for decades. The Web has only made this deception easier both because of the availability of information, as well as the kinds of personal information that can be accessed if one hacks into a computer system.

Today people who want to find out more information about others may start by visiting popular Internet search engines like Google or Yahoo! and typing in a person's name. Although not everyone's information can be found on the Web, this kind of data is available for many people. Anyone who searches is likely to find out what organizations someone belongs to as well as his or her home address and phone number. Closely tied to the rise of the Internet has been an increase in the proliferation of and access to personal information. In the early days of the Internet, many users unknowingly released confidential information for public consumption, and organizations published details about their members that many thought at the time were innocuous. In cases where this information isn't available free of charge, such as credit and criminal background checks, it can often be found for a small fee.

Over time, people realized that some of this information violated the privacy guarantees of individuals, or that members of organizations did not feel comfortable about their organizations releasing this information. Increased online commerce has also meant that people are now using their credit cards with more frequency. This has led relatively sophisticated networks of criminals to establish realistic-looking, but phony, Web sites that are simply used to gather important (often financial) information from consumers. Also, small-time foreign gangs have been luring some Internet users to participate in frauds and scams that allow the gangs to steal the financial information or hard-earned assets of their victims. This practice, often called identity theft, can cause long-term damage to a person's creditworthiness. Typically, it is very difficult to resurrect or repair credit-related identity once it has been stolen. Finally, with the rise of personal Web sites, blogs, and social networking sites such as Facebook and MySpace, it has become even easier to acquire more information about others.

SPOOFING

Another scam, called "spoofing," is when someone receives an e-mail that appears to be from a legitimate source but turns out to have been sent by someone else. The source of the e-mail might seem to be a credit card company, bank, or online auction site informing the recipient that there has been some suspicious activity on their account. Victims of spoofing may be asked to call a phone number or, more typically, are advised to visit a Web site and provide their e-mail address, credit card information, and personal data such as passwords, mailing address, and even the names of their children. These e-mails aren't legitimate; users who aren't careful may not even realize they've been scammed until the crooks have used their personal data to purchase items or services with their credit card or withdraw money from their bank account.

PHISHING

Similar to spoofing, phishing occurs when a perpetrator collects or purchases a significant number of e-mail addresses and then sends his targets an official sounding and looking e-mail that appears to be from a well known corporation, like a financial institution, or a Web site, such as Amazon, eBay, or Hotmail. The e-mail claims that there has been some sort of security breach on the victims' account, and in order to rectify the problem and prevent the account being closed or being responsible for additional charges, they must provide confidential information such as their credit card number, Social Security number, or password. Alternatively, the potential or actual victim may be redirected to an official-looking Web site, which displays a form that captures the same kind of information.

Many people have learned to recognize possible phishing attempts because these e-mails often contain poor grammar and spelling. Other clues include an entire subject line in capital letters that might state "URGENT REPLY NEEDED," which is a giveaway that something is fishy. Unfortunately, all sorts of financial institutions and consumers have been hit by this kind of scam.

Phishing scams typically require users to log on to an authentic-looking Web site that mimics one from an organization or company with which they may do business. These sites tend to look sophisticated and often closely resemble a company's or an organization's actual Web site. Phishing scams often rely upon spoofing to draw in unsuspecting computer users, and they most likely also incorporate fake return addresses in the e-mail solicitation that appear to be legitimate. After a user has entered his or her personal information, it may then become evident that the site isn't legitimate after all. This is precisely why many computer users will not open e-mails from individuals and organizations they do not know. It is also why some companies will block attachments from outside users. "Messagelabs, a leading provider of managed e-mail security services to businesses worldwide, reportedly detects 80–100 new phishing Web sites each day, which shows how ubiquitous this form of cybercrime has become."[1] Because of phishing scams, many companies also now state on their official Web sites that they will never ask users to reveal their password. In many respects, phishing is a modern-day form of counterfeiting.

Estimates regarding the amount of dollar loss as a result of phishing in the United States range between $137 and $500 million. Approximately 3 percent of all people who are exposed to phishing scams end up being victimized.

PHARMING

Two other variants of phishing include identity theft through DNS cache poisoning (pharming) and identity theft through spyware. In the first instance, the Web user logs on to a purported Web site only to immediately be redirected to another site. In effect, the legitimate site has been altered by the cybercriminal in order to redirect the unsuspecting visitor to a phony one. With respect to the second, in order to properly visit many Web sites computer browsers need to have their cookies enabled. This allows all sorts of codes to be transferred from one computer to another. Most of these codes are safe, but some can be malicious, like spyware. The spyware can collect information from users, including their keystrokes, which is then sent back through the Internet to a mainframe. "Once the specialist malicious software . . . has infected a computer, it harvests information and returns it to the infector.[2] Another way to fall victim to these kinds of codes is to surf the Web and install what appear to be anti-spyware programs on a computer. These are sometimes used to dupe people into using harmful software.

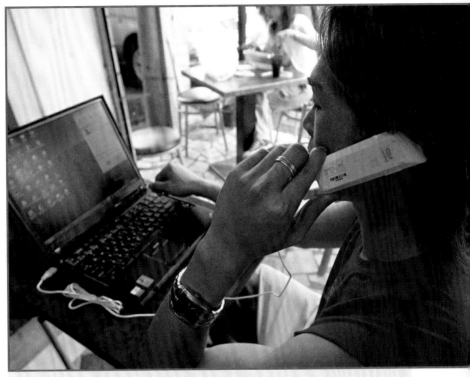

A man uses a Skype Internet phone to make a call. In recent years, Skype technology has become a popular means for criminals to commit identity theft. *Richard Chung/Reuters/Corbis*

VISHING

In 2006 cyber cops began to notice modifications to the traditional phishing scams. These computer crimes were labeled *vishing* and *smishing*. The former consists of using VoIP (Voice over Internet Protocol) "to 'spam' recorded messages to telephone numbers rather than e-mails. . . . The VoIP messages purport to be from" financial institutions or other businesses and, like the traditional phishers, suggest to the recipient that their credit cards have been used improperly.[3] Using Skype technology, the perpetrator either calls stolen numbers or goes through the phone book and leaves prerecorded messages indicating that a fraud-detection service has indicated that the recipient has incurred unauthorized charges on a credit card. The victim is instructed to call a number, and he or she is then asked to provide all sorts of personal information. If they do so, they become a victim of identity theft.

SMISHING

Smishing is a variant of phishing that occurs via cell phone text messaging. A perpetrator sends a message asking the recipient to reveal confidential personal information through either a Web site or by calling a phone number. These communications are often alarmist in nature; the content might state that the message is meant to confirm a service order that was actually never placed. The text will then refer the recipient to a phone number or a Web site where he or she must enter personal information to correct the "erroneous" order. The message is designed to create a state of alarm or panic in someone with the hope that he or she will rush to a phone, contact the number provided, and reveal the private information.

Cyberstalking and Cyberbullying

In 1996 Jayne Hitchcock continuously received numerous and similar e-mails, called a mail bomb attack, from a literary agent after she had posted negative information about bad dealings with the agency on a public Web site. One could understand several e-mail messages from the aggrieved party, but it was more than a few. These actions overloaded Hitchcock's e-mail account and continued even when she changed her e-mail address. After a protracted legal battle, the spate of e-mails subsided, and Hitchcock wrote a book based on her experience titled *Net Crimes and Misdemeanors*. Hitchcock has used her experience to become an expert on cyberstalking and bullying. Her work also helped both California and Maryland pass anti-cyberstalking legislation.

Increasingly, the public and law enforcement agencies are recognizing that the Internet is being used to intimidate or harass individuals and organizations. This problem cannot be easily ignored. Many well-known incidents of cyberstalking and cyberbullying have occurred in the United States and elsewhere through blogs and social networking Web sites such as MySpace and Facebook. Average citizens and celebrities have become victims and have had malicious or damaging information about them revealed on these sites. Another danger is that pedophiles use the World Wide Web to find and lure underage children in an attempt to have sex with them.

CYBERSTALKING

Although the Internet has improved people's ability and speed to communicate with one another, it has also facilitated the harassment of individuals and organizations. When this behavior is persistent and threatening it is typically called cyberstalking.[1] Harassment can include impersonating another individual or sending numerous e-mail messages, spam, and malware to an individual or organization.[2] Naturally, there is a distinction between nuisance and harassment; sometimes this perception depends on how victims interpret the unwanted attention and communications. In other words, harassment is often in the eye of the beholder.

Certain actions are easier to define as cyberstalking if the victim has asked the stalker to cease and desist but the actions continue. Cyberstalking can be accompanied by solicitations for sex, threats of violence, accusations, and identity theft. Cyberstalking can even escalate to physical stalking and assault. Cyberstalking begins with the perpetrator gathering information about the intended victim from a variety of sources. The information is then used to monitor, threaten, and harass the victim via the Internet or World Wide Web. This can include e-mails or posting false information on the Internet or World Wide Web.[3]

Two notable cases of cyberstalking led to convictions of the perpetrators. In 1996, University of California, Irvine, student Richard Machado sent hate e-mail that threatened to kill Asian students. He was eventually arrested, charged, and convicted of civil rights violations. Machado was the first person in the United States to be convicted in federal courts of using the Internet to harass others. In 1998, Kingman Quon, a college student from Corona, California, sent numerous death threats to Hispanic professors and students all around the United States. Like Machado, he was arrested, charged, and convicted of violating the civil rights of his victims because of their ethnicity or national origin. These two cases are but the tip of the iceberg of ongoing federal cases involving hate messages sent through the Internet.

Cyberstalking can also involve a unique situation in which someone purchases the naming rights to the Web sites of deceased or victimized individuals. In the United States there have been a handful of sites named after victims of brutal crimes, sometimes created by the actual or alleged perpetrators of those illegal actions. These are not memorial sites; they are designed to harass the loved ones of the victims by being a constant reminder of the crime. The parents of the victim usually try to claim the rights to the site through a court order or a defamation suit but are often unsuccessful. This is a variant of cybersquatting (also known as domain squatting), where individuals purchase a domain name that matches an existing business name or trademark with the intent to sell it at a higher price to that person or organization in the future. This practice led to the passage of the Anticybersquatting Consumer Protection Act in 1999 as well as other similar laws at the state and federal level.

Both spammers and stalkers have found numerous ways to outsmart their victims and authorities. One such technique involves relying on remailers to ensure anonymity. "Remailers are computer services which cloak the identity of users who send messages through stripping all identifying information from an e-mail and allocating an 'anonymous ID'."[4] One such remailer site is http://www.anonymizer.com. Although anonymity can protect criminals, there are also arguments in favor of it: "Anonymity is . . . Important for on-line discussions and newsgroups dealing with sensitive issues such as sexual abuse, domestic violence, and alcoholism. . . . Anonymity can also facilitate the protection of privacy on the Internet."[5]

INTERNET GROOMING

Cyberstalking should be distinguished from Internet grooming, which involves a person cultivating an individual, typically an underage minor, online for later exploitation offline. One of the more well-known cases involved Toby Studabaker, a 31-year-old U.S. Marine who, after a relatively brief online exchange with a 12-year-old British girl, arranged to meet her in person in Paris, France, and abducted her. Studabaker, a pedophile, wanted to have sex with an underage child. He was eventually tracked down in Frankfurt, Germany, arrested, and prosecuted. It is argued that his case led to the United Kingdom's passage of the *Sexual Offences Act.*[6]

CYBERBULLYING

Before the Internet existed personal ads were sometimes used as a relatively easy and cheap way to bully, embarrass, or make fun of another person. Today bullying has moved from the printed page to cyberspace. This can include repeated e-mail or text messaging contact with an individual who wants no further contact, spreading malicious information about that person on social networking sites, threatening others, and revealing personal and confidential information about that person, including his or her contact information. Whether or not this can legitimately be considered a crime is hard to determine. Unlike in the past, the Internet has made it easier for cyberbullies to remain anonymous.

Communication among friends, relatives, and associates is easier thanks to the advance of social networking Web sites. Facebook, for example, allows members to stay in touch with their network through a platform that includes instant messaging and e-mail. Facebook permits its users to post written communications, photographs, and videos. It serves as a mechanism where those in a network can not only compliment other people but also criticize them online, too. Facebook members can also use an application that allows users to post messages through an *honesty box*, which allows posters to leave anonymous comments for people in their network. Users who install the honesty box on their Facebook page can ask a question such as "What is one thing that you don't like about me?" If they are not prepared for the responses, it can be damaging to their friendships.

Cyberbullying is not restricted to the computer. It can also include cell phones through text messaging, or blocking the caller ID function before making bullying calls. It also occurs through submissions to YouTube. Jilted boyfriends and girlfriends can post videos that reflect negatively on their former close friends. Cyberbullying can even involve any combination of these technologies.

During the 1990s, especially because of the rise of social networking Web sites, there were many news stories about cyberbullying. In Vermont in 2003, for example, 13-year-old Ryan Patrick Halligan hung himself after being subjected to repeated instant messaging (IM) and Internet bullying. Over a period of a year, Halligan received taunts that made fun of his learning disorder and implied that he was gay. One cyberbully, in particular, created an intricate plan that involved a girl Halligan liked pretending to be interested in him, only to later publicly embarrass him. The bullying seemed to ebb and flow for a time but increased in the summer of 2003 just before Halligan took his own life.

Another well-known case of cyberbullying that had a devastating outcome involved the suicide of 13-year-old Megan Meier, from Missouri. In 2006 Lori Drew, the mother of one of Meier's former

John Halligan shows the Web page devoted to his son, Ryan, who committed suicide in 2003 after enduring months of online bullying.
AP Photo/Toby Talbot

friends, posed as a 16-year-old boy named Josh Evans and created a fake MySpace account under his name. Numerous people in Meier's circle of acquaintances knew of the fictitious account and contributed to the posts. An employee of Drew's, Ashley Grills, wrote one of the final messages on the account and told Meier that the world would be a better place without her. Shortly after receiving the message, Meier, who had a history of psychiatric problems, committed suicide. When word got out and authorities examined Meier's MySpace account, they discovered Drew's deception. Prosecutors charged Drew with four felonies that included violating the federal *Computer Fraud and Abuse Act*. As a result of the trial, the jury concluded that Drew was not guilty of a felony charge, but they convicted her of misdemeanor charges of computer fraud.

PROLIFERATION OF HATE VIA THE INTERNET

The Web has fostered the dissemination of offensive communication, including words and images, as well as hard-core, violent, and child pornography. Some of the most controversial communications, however, involve hate speech. Hate speech includes sending or posting information that is biased, degrading, or incendiary in nature directed toward a particular race, ethnicity, religion, gender, or nationality. A considerable amount of this offensive communication on the Web is typically racist in nature. Because free speech is protected by the First Amendment of the U.S. constitution, it is possible for hate speech to appear on the Web.

The Web has allowed individuals and organizations to disseminate information and engage in harmful actions and devices. This is done through a variety of Web-based dissemination vehicles such as Web sites, groups, chats, and blogs that provide information and offer advice on everything from constructing weapons (bombs) to committing all sorts of crimes.

Certainly, the communication advantages of the Web have allowed hate speech to proliferate. Based on research by Laura Nielsen, "Hate speech can be defined as 'speech that (1) has a message of racial inferiority, (2) is directed against a member of a historically oppressed group, and (3) is persecutory, hateful and degrading.'"[7]

One of the most notorious cases of disseminating hate speech on the Web involves Ernest Zundel. A German-born printer who moved to Toronto, Canada, in 1958, Zundel was a well-known Holocaust denier. He and others are part of a small group of individuals who not only question the facts surrounding the Holocaust

Tina Meier holds two pictures of her daughter Megan, who committed suicide in October 2006 after receiving cruel messages on MySpace. *AP Photo/Tom Gannam*

(i.e., the intentional genocide of German and other European Jews by the Nazi regime during World War II), but claim that it never took place. In the early part of his career, he started printing tracts that denied the Holocaust and blamed Jews for all sorts of things. Over the years, he progressed to posting and distributing his rants online. As news about his writings got out, he increasingly became the target of law enforcement, media attention, the B'nai B'rith organization (an organization that campaigns against anti-Semitism), and even some bombings. His supporters included neo-Nazis, extreme right-wingers, and civil libertarians who wanted to protect Zundel's right to free speech. Zundel's detractors saw his reliance on this right as a ploy to hide his anti-Semitism.

The Zundel case, and similar incidents throughout Western countries, prompted the creation of hate crime legislation; a mechanism for legally holding individuals accountable for malicious acts directed at individuals because of their race, ethnicity, sexual preference, or national origin. As hate crime legislation evolved in Canada, Zundel was constantly in and out of court and spent some time in jail. Zundel moved to the United States but was arrested and deported back to Canada when his visa expired. He was then extradited to Germany because of irregularities in his immigration paperwork. Because Zundel broke German laws by sending his publications to Germany and because he remained a German citizen, he was convicted and sentenced to jail. He remains incarcerated in a German correctional facility on violation of hate speech laws in that country, where Holocaust denial is illegal.

Since the 1960s most industrialized democracies have criminalized hate speech, yet there are numerous Web sites and chat sites devoted to hate topics. This is because banning hate speech can be seen as censorship. Some have argued that there is a fine line between hate speech and free speech.

DIFFICULT ISSUES

Cyberbullying and cyberstalking appear to be on the rise. The difficult issues for those trying to deal with it, such as parents, teachers, criminal justice practitioners, and others, is to determine when communications are simply the exercise of an individual's right to free speech and when it passes the threshold into bullying or stalking.

Most western countries have established legislation or have embedded in their constitutions strong freedom of speech guarantees. These must be balanced against the harm done to an identifiable group. When the harm moves from speech to physical action, then it is easier for law enforcement to intervene. Unfortunately this often occurs too late, and needless suffering, injury, and possible death might occur in the meantime.

Online Pornography

The Web and the invention of reasonably priced, user-friendly, sophisticated digital cameras have made pornography much more readily available to the average computer user. In fact, the pornography industry is one of the biggest content providers on the Web, which has affected supply, demand, and so-called creativity.[1] The Internet is also being used as a conduit for prostitutes, pimps, and customers to conduct business. There are not only numerous Web sites specifically devoted to pornography, but also multipurpose sites such as Craigslist, the popular and free classified ad sales Web site, that are used for this sort of business.

One of the biggest problems with pornographic material on the Internet is that it's difficult to prevent children from accessing it. This is why many pornographic Web sites show warning labels that indicate users under the age of 18 may not enter the site or that users enter at their own risk. However, these do not actually prevent the user from accessing the site. Additionally, parents or other responsible adults such as schoolteachers and administrators can set Web browsers to block certain sites and prevent access by children. Software programs are available that filter out and block potentially offensive sites, but they sometimes also block useful sites.

THE GROWTH OF ONLINE PORNOGRAPHY

Since the invention of the World Wide Web, the number and type of pornography Web sites has increased steadily. Based on online requests, users can find photos and videos, including real-time, streaming videos. There is a wide variety of content. Samples of this pornographic content are often free, though users must eventually pay to gain access to additional or so-called higher-quality content. Some Internet experts have suggested that the rise of online pornography was the catalyst behind other businesses, such as Netflix or Blockbuster, offering popular movies as "streaming" videos for purchase via the Web.

Another important issue is the consensual nature of pornography. It is difficult, if not impossible, for viewers to determine whether or not the photos and videos were taken with the subject's, model's, or performer's permission to distribute them publicly for a profit. In order for pornography to be legal, the individuals depicted in the images must have agreed that their pictures can be taken and posted on the Web. Most studies have determined that the majority of pornographic material is developed with the consent of the actors or models who appear in it. Acts that are not consensual include acts with children, mentally disturbed or incapacitated individuals, and animals. Also, contemporary legal documents have defined actions that are considered obscene under any circumstances. These include nonconsensual behaviors such as sexual acts with children, sexual assaults on children, the portrayal of incest, sex with an animal, rape, taking drugs, flagellation, torture, bondage, dismemberment, cannibalism, and consuming bodily wastes.

Pornographers have used legal defenses against charges of pornography, including the right to free speech. Over the last decade, U.S. courts have applied the test of lasciviousness (e.g., excessive sexual desire) to determine whether something is indeed pornographic.

Child pornography. The Internet allows those with an interest in viewing child pornography to gain quick access to this kind of illegal content from one's home or office. According to Wall, "At the core of public and legal concerns about child pornography is the ability of investigators and prosecutors to determine when imagery contravenes the law."[2] In order to skirt the issue of using real children, pornographers started using what are called "pseudo photographs." These are images that were not taken directly with a camera, but have been enhanced in some shape or manner, sometimes through the use of Adobe Photoshop software, to make the image appear as if it depicts a child. They are illegal.

Violent imagery: sexual and nonsexual. Starting in the 1990s, critics of Web-based pornography began to voice concerns

Detectives stand over evidence seized during a child pornography investigation in Ontario, Canada, in July 2006. *AP Photo/CP, Aaron Harris*

about sexually violent images and videos on the Internet, including snuff movies (which purport to depict a person being killed). Most law enforcement authorities claim that almost all of these acts are staged. Some of this violent imagery has emerged due to the Iraq War, the War on Terror, and the invention of YouTube. YouTube, a popular Web site for the transmission of short digital video content, has become a prominent vehicle for distributing these sorts of videos. Following the Iraq War (2003–present), videos of individuals being decapitated by Islamic terrorists began being posted online. "Unlike the snuff movies, which were designed to be sold, these execution videos are primarily instruments of cyber-terror, because they are intended to further the makers' political agenda, spreading fear and outrage across the victims' communities, while galvanizing their own supporters."[3]

Law enforcement attempts to combat pornography.
In the United States, legislation exists to sanction individuals and organizations that manufacture and distribute child pornography. These are embedded in two federal statutes: The Protection of Children against Sexual Exploitation Act (1977) and The Child Protection and Obscenity Enforcement Act (1988). This legislation is fortified by the Communication Decency Act (1996) and the Child Pornography Prevention Act (1996).

Among the different kinds of cybercrime that exist in the world today, child pornography appears to generate a considerable amount of cooperation among law enforcement organizations in different countries trying to combat it. Three combined operations include the 1995 investigation and arrest of individuals in connection with Operation Starburst. This included the participation of law enforcement agencies in the United States, South Africa, Europe, and Southeast Asia. In 1998 police in the United Kingdom, with the assistance of law enforcement in the United States and Interpol, broke up the Wonderland Club, a group that distributed child pornography online. And in 2003 Operation Ore took place with the cooperation of British and American Law enforcement. In each case more than 30 men were arrested. Identifying and arresting these criminals often this involves tracking the credit card information of the perpetrators.

Connecticut state Attorney General Richard Blumenthal (right) makes a point as Craigslist CEO Jim Buckmaster looks on at a news conference in Hartford, Connecticut, in November 2008. Blumenthal announced that Connecticut and 39 other states have reached an agreement with Craigslist under which the online classified advertisement Web site will act to crack down on ads for prostitution. *AP Photo/Bob Child*

USE OF THE INTERNET FOR PROSTITUTION

The Internet has made it easier for prostitutes, pimps, and clients to do their illegal business. There are Web sites where potential customers can view prostitutes, purchase services, and even rank the women (or men) that they solicit. According to Sharpe and Earle, there are three basic types of prostitutes who advertise over the Web: First are the "high-end" escort services advertising their employees and allowing their clients to rank their services. The sites make it explicit that the hourly rates only involve "spending time" with a service provider and do not entail sex. However, any discerning viewer knows that this is not the case. Second are the independents, which work alone, are not part of an agency, and may rely upon posting pornographic photos to attract customers. Finally, there are massage parlors. These sites may depict the actual facility and provide directions. Some Web sites, such as Craigslist, offer a category called "casual encounters" within the personals section. Though it isn't clearly stated, it's widely known that this section is used for the solicitation of prostitutes.[4] These postings came under close scrutiny in 2009 after a series of cases emerged in which meetings arranged through such ads resulted in murders.

The information highway is a means of free speech. As a result it offers a way for some people to obtain pornography, whether legal or illegal, and for others to meet someone for purposes of paid sex. This presents a real problem for law enforcement in combating illegal activities of this type, the human trafficking in women to be used as prostitutes, as well as those connected with displaying sexually charged photos or videos that involve minors.

Responding
to Cybercrime

Every few years stories surface about how cyber detectives manage to solve particularly complicated cases. One of the most well known is Tsutomu Shimomura, a physics engineer and computer security expert, who in 1995 was important in detecting and capturing cybercriminal Kevin Mitnick. Having illegally gained access to several computer systems (including one managed by the Department of Defense), stolen computer programs, and used long distance networks without paying for them, Mitnick was being watched by the Federal Bureau of Investigation. Mitnick, however, made the mistake of trying to enter Shimomura's computer account. Shimomura made it his personal mission to track down Mitnick. Shimomura's exploits tracking Mitnick are documented in his 1996 book, *Takedown: The Pursuit and Capture of Kevin Mitnick, America's Most Wanted Computer Outlaw-By the Man Who Did It*, co-authored with journalist John Markoff.

Sir Isaac Newton, the famous physicist, is well known for his law that states that for every action there is an equal and opposite reaction. In general, this process has been true for those who are responsible for and make their living protecting individuals, organizations, corporations, and the government from cybercrime. It often seems that no sooner than computer professionals detect a new malware and create a patch enabling computer systems to properly function, that the hackers and malware writers strike back with a new way to compromise the security of computers or launch a new virus, Trojan horse, or worm. But who are these people who come to our rescue and what kinds of tools do they have at their disposal?

Tsutomo Shimomura works on his laptop in February 1996. Shimomura was a key figure in detecting and capturing cybercriminal Kevin Mitnick in 1995. *Najlah Feanny/Corbis Saba*

Moreover, what sorts of preventive measures can the general public take to minimize becoming a victim of cybercrime?

In recent years there has been a proliferation of protocols, practices, products, laws, individuals, and businesses that have been established to minimize or respond to the threat of cybercrime. This also includes efforts to fight cybercrime at the local, state, federal, and international levels.

RESPONDING TO HACKING AND CYBERTERRORISM

In response to the threat of hacking and cyberterrorism, many advanced industrialized democracies have invested a considerable amount of resources into protecting their country's critical information infrastructure. In the United States, for example, $1.5 billion was allocated to shore up cyber security during the Clinton Administration. During this time a comprehensive plan called *Defending America's Cyberspace: National Plan for Information Systems Protection* was written. The report, which depended on the input of major government entities, had three basic objectives: "prevent cyber attacks against America's critical infrastructures; reduce national vulnerability to cyber attacks; and minimize damage and recovery time from cyber attacks that do occur."[1] In so doing, the study surveyed the importance of cyber security at that time in the United States. It also outlined what the authors believed was the government's responsibility of ensuring cyber security. Further action was taken during the Bush administration with the release of the report, *National Strategy to Secure Cyberspace* in 2003, and money then budgeted for cyber security was $839.3 billion.

COMBATING CYBERCRIME

Looking at this phenomenon in a more general sense, there are three strategies to minimize online fraud: legislative harmonization, centralized reporting and coordination, and specialized training and coordination in law enforcement.[2] Several professions now have a role in the detection and prevention of cybercrime, and the prosecution of individuals and/or criminal organizations that engage in it. Computer security specialists routinely create lists of what they believe are the key ways that computer users (and Internet users in particular) can avoid or minimize the risk of becoming victims of computer crime. These suggestions are available on the Internet and in information technology (IT) magazines (See Box, page 92).

Most of this information, like wearing a seatbelt when driving a vehicle, is just plain common sense. What may be more interesting is why computer users choose to ignore these precautions. But this is a subject best left for a different venue. At the very least, most computer and software manufacturers recommend users update software on a regular basis. Almost all software includes a mechanism that allows users to opt in to have software automatically updated with security patches over the Internet. Beyond this advice are other helpful tips. For example, it is not wise to keep one's computer on for long periods of time. Users may think that this prevents the hassle of starting the computer up again. However, if the computer has an Internet connection, it is more likely to be compromised by hackers the longer it is connected to the Internet. Hackers can penetrate or slow down the system by piggybacking on it.

Education. Unfortunately the average computer user and most criminal justice practitioners are inadequately prepared for detecting cybercrime and appropriately responding to allegations of cybercrime. Although the subject of cybercrime is being introduced into community colleges, universities, and in-service training for law enforcement professionals, most security experts admit

♀ BASIC TIPS FOR MINIMIZING RISK OF CYBERCRIME

1. Make sure to use encryption for wireless connections.
2. Keep operating systems such as Windows updated at all times.
3. Ensure that virus protection software (for example McAfee, Norton Utilities) is updated at all times.
4. Do not give out passwords.
5. Change passwords on a regular basis.
6. Avoid using simple passwords; use a combination of letters, numbers, and symbols.
7. Make sure a firewall is activated.
8. Do not keep a computer on while unattended for long periods of time.
9. Clean out registry cache and temporary Internet files on a regular basis.
10. Consult a professional or use a commercial hard drive sanitizing program when disposing of a computer or hard drive.

there is a long way to go toward providing proper education and training.

In an attempt to improve this state of affairs, the federal government has instituted the Federal Cyber Service: Scholarship for Service program. For several years the National Science Foundation, one of the most prestigious scientific organizations in the United States, "has collaborated with the National Security Agency (NSA) to improve course, curriculum, instructional materials, and computer forensics laboratories in order to better educate and train the next-generation of cyber investigators and information security specialists, and to prepare them for protecting organizations, communities, and the national critical information infrastructure from cyber attacks. Over fifty universities are now certified by NSA as Centers of Academic Excellence providing information security specialists and investigators."[3]

Detection. Detection of sophisticated computer crimes is typically a job for experts in computer forensic science. In this case, the role of first responders in the detection of computer crime cannot be overemphasized. First responders need to be properly trained to secure computers and other electronic devices as evidence so that information can be protected in order to secure a conviction. "Electronic evidence is defined as information and data of investigative value stored on or transmitted by an electronic device. As such, electronic evidence is latent evidence. In its natural state, we cannot 'see' what is contained in the physical object that holds the evidence, much the same as fingerprints or DNA."[4] The problem for investigators and crooks alike is that electronic evidence is not visible to the eye and thus it makes it difficult both to observe it and also to destroy it.

The role of first responders. In terms of detection, many precautions must be taken by first responders at crime scenes where electronic devices, in addition to computers, are collected as evidence. First, one must recognize the range of electronic devices that can assist in an investigation, including answering machines and digital cameras. These items may have important information stored on them that would provide law enforcement and prosecutors enough incriminating evidence to arrest and bring charges against an individual or an organization, successfully prosecute them, and convict the perpetrators.

Confiscated computers and child-oriented pornographic tapes fill the storeroom shelves in the Florida Attorney General's Child Predator Cybercrime Unit office in Jacksonville, Florida. It is important for law-enforcement officials to be extremely careful and thorough in gathering and cataloguing evidence when investigating the "scene" of a cybercrime. *AP Photo/Oscar Sosa*

PDAs, pagers, cell phones, printers, copiers, GPS devices, and compact flash devices may have important incriminating information stored on them. In general, law enforcement officers are the ones who must secure the evidence. This includes properly labeling, packaging, transporting, and storing electronic devices and any other material gathered as evidence.

Problems with arresting, prosecuting, and convicting cybercriminals. It can be difficult to carry out arrests, prosecutions, and convictions for cybercrime. Part of the reason why is that the perpetrators often live in different states and/or countries than their victims, and appropriate law enforcement response requires coordination on a national and/or international level among criminal justice personnel. Also, it can be difficult to get local police to investigate cybercrimes because they either lack the resources, the necessary sophisticated training, or the desire needed to investigate and understand cybercrimes. Also, if it is not clear that the crime occurred in their jurisdiction, they may think that they are not the appropriate agency to investigate it.

As a partial response to this challenge, many law enforcement agencies and large corporations are starting computer crime divisions. Since the 1980s the FBI, for example, has had a very powerful and well-known Computer Analysis and Response Team (CART).

Many countries and regions have established agencies either for the coordination of cybercrime investigations, or for the dissemination of information related to cybercrime. One such agency is the European Union's high-tech crime agency, ENISA. Launched in 2004, it is responsible for coordinating investigations into cybercrime by police in member countries and disseminating information about threats. According to ENISA's Web site, the agency monitors threats to the communications systems in the EU member countries. It also publishes a journal that informs its member countries about trends in cybercrime and efforts to combat it.

Tools of the trade. Computer forensic investigators now have at their disposal a number of important diagnostic tools to detect an attack and isolate cybercrime. As the Mitnick and Shimomura case illustrate, there is a considerable amount of hype, however, about the powers of cyber detectives and cyber forensics.

Basic investigation process. When determining whether or not someone might be a suspect, police often consider if the person had the means, motive, and opportunity to commit the crime. Computer security expert Don Parker developed the idea of SKRAM to apply to cybercrime. This is an acronym for the *s*kills, *k*nowledge, *r*esources, technical *a*uthority, and *m*otive required to commit the crime. This model is helpful for detectives and cyber security professionals to focus on individuals and organizations who might be suspected cybercriminals by determining if they meet the requirements of SKRAM. It can be implemented before, during, or after a cyberattack.

A major difficulty in detecting and responding to cybercriminals is lack of money, personnel, and skills among law enforcement and

♀ TSUTOMU SHIMOMURA

Tsutomu Shimomura, a Japanese-American scientist and computer security expert, helped the FBI track down and arrest hacker Kevin Mitnick. In 1995, Shimomura, while working, noticed that someone had hacked his computer using an IP spoofing attack. The hack was later tracked to Mitnick, who was well known to police and the FBI for prior convictions as a juvenile for hacking into multiple computer systems. The Mitnick/Shimomura case has been a story in itself. No less than two books have been written about the capture of Mitnick. They include *Takedown* by Shimomura and John Markoff and *The Fugitive Game* by Jonathan Littman, which challenges some of the assertions in *Takedown*. Some individuals familiar with the case have alleged that Shimomura's book embellished on many details of the pursuit. Mitnick's book, *The Art of Deception*, also discusses the case.

security professionals. "For example, the UK's National Hi-Tech Crime Unit was established in 2001, comprising 80 dedicated officers and with a budget of £25 million; however, this amounts to less than 0.1 percent of the total number of police, and less than 0.5 percent over the overall expenditure on 'reduction of crime.'"[5]

Peter Grabosky and Russell Smith, Australian criminologists, suggest "that much computer-related illegality lies beyond the capacity of contemporary law enforcement and regulatory agencies alone to control, and that security in cyberspace will depend on the efforts of a wide range of institutions, as well as on a degree of self-help by potential victims of digital crime. The ideal configuration may be expected to differ, depending upon the activity in question, but it is likely to entail a mix of law enforcement, technological and market solutions."[6]

INADEQUACY OF EXISTING LAWS AND THE NEED FOR NEW LAWS

In the early years of prosecution against hackers, legal systems depended on charging perpetrators with criminal trespass, violating the private property guarantees of individuals and organizations. As prosecutors failed to secure convictions, however, it became clear that existing criminal laws were insufficient or not specific enough. One of the first countries to introduce a law related to computer crime was the United States. In 1986 Congress passed the Computer Fraud and Abuse Act (CFAA). It "made it a crime to 'knowingly access computers without authorization, obtain unauthorized information with intent to defraud, or 'cause damage' to 'protected computers.'"[7] This law imposes sentences of five years for first time offenders and 10 years for repeat offenders. The CFAA has been amended several times, and there are similar kinds of legislation at the state levels.

In 1996 the federal government passed the Communications Decency Act (CDA), the first notable attempt by the U.S. Congress to monitor pornography on the Internet. In 1997 the Supreme Court partially overturned the act, because it impinged on the constitutionally protected right to free speech. What remained intact were sections which protected **Internet Service Providers** (ISPs) from prosecution and limited their liability when offensive communications were sent over their systems. On the heels of the CDA came attempts to pass a cyberstalking law at the federal level. Individual states followed with their own cyberstalking laws. States are in different stages of passage of this legislation.

The United Kingdom (England, Wales, Scotland, and Northern Ireland) relies upon the Computer Misuse Act of 1990 to prosecute cybercriminals. If this act is insufficient to prosecute an alleged perpetrator then the government can rely on the Telecommunications Act.

No data exists in the United Kingdom or the United States on how successful this legislation is in deterring, capturing, or prosecuting cybercriminals. Moreover, these kinds of laws have been criticized by many people and organizations. One of the most common criticisms is that perpetrators are rarely prosecuted to the full extent of the law and their punishments often amount to a slap on the wrist. "Numerous types of cybercrime, if they originated in the United States and involve computer systems of the federal government, are now, under provisions of the USA Patriot Act and other federal crime laws, considered felonies or even acts of terrorism."[8]

The Patriot Act, passed in 2001, significantly enabled the U.S. government to search its citizens's e-mail communications and thus reduced constitutionally mandated provisions on Americans right to privacy.

Each country has different laws regarding cybercrimes. Some attempts at coordinating laws internationally have been conducted, but it will be a long time before uniform laws are applied to all sorts of computer crimes. Most nations are still catching up. New and evolving computer crimes are developed quicker than legislation can be created and appropriate investigative agencies established.

In many, if not most cases of computer crime, the perpetrator lives and works in one country and the victim is in another. This can be a blessing and a curse. It can benefit perpetrators because the distance involved can be a disincentive for victims and law enforcement agencies to investigate and prosecute perpetrators. Also, the laws and criminal justice practices in the criminal's country may not be developed enough to secure a conviction. On the other hand, the fact that more than one jurisdiction is involved has enabled prosecutors to shop for an appropriate venue (i.e., place) for pressing charges. This practice, called "forum-shopping," lets prosecutors find the most favorable jurisdiction for securing a conviction. Prosecutors in the United States have tried cases in states that are more amenable to prosecution and have chosen between countries, for example the United States versus Nigeria, where a conviction of some sort is less likely.

PROBLEMS WITH PROSECUTION

It appears that there is a gap between the number of cybercrimes reported each year and the number of people actually convicted. This phenomenon has to do in part with the slippery legal definitions of cybercrime and the relative lack of resources and inexperience of criminal justice system practitioners with new types of cybercrime. For example, the media sometimes reports stories about private organizations like Perverted Justice or law enforcement sting operations designed to catch individuals using the Internet to lure young girls or boys away from home for the purposes of sex. In these sting operations police officers often pose as young girls or boys online to engage deviants in illegal actions. These law enforcement techniques are often controversial and seen as exercises in entrapment.

This basically means that law enforcement agents are coercing individuals to commit a crime that under normal circumstances they would never do, although Perverted Justice claims they wait for the target of their sting to initiate inappropriate contact.

Dateline NBC has frequently run a newsmagazine show called *To Catch a Predator* in which volunteers from Perverted Justice pose via the Internet as underage boys or girls and then lure pedophiles into meeting with someone they believe is a minor. When the alleged perpetrator arrives at the designated meeting site, he or she is greeted by a news team with cameras rolling and often police officers ready to arrest the perpetrator. The show was cancelled in 2008. The efforts of the show led to many convictions, but in many cases charges against the targets were dropped over various legal concerns.

PREVENTION

Numerous controls and protections against cybercrime exist. They may not lead to the elimination of cybercrime, but they will help diminish its proliferation or reduce having individuals or businesses victimized. Internet service providers can self-regulate by instituting protocols or policies against certain kinds of content. Not all kinds of controls, however, work everywhere. In other words, one size does not fit all. Therefore, fighting cybercrime takes a range of protections.

Virus detection software. The existence of malware such as viruses, Trojan horses, and worms has led to the proliferation of tools that prevent computer systems from being infected. Over the past two decades we have witnessed the manufacture, marketing, purchase, and use of privacy and malware detection software. These include commercial products from companies like McAfee and Norton Utilities that detect, block, or remove malware. Free tools, such as Adware, Lavasoft, or Malwarebytes, are also available on the Internet. Computer users must be careful before downloading these kinds of tools. Some are hoaxes that may either take users' money or cause their computer to become infected.

Hotlines. Another control against cybercrime, at least in the case of pornography, is the establishment of hotlines to report inappropriate content. These "have been promoted by the European Union's Action Plan, and the UK Internet Watch Foundation (IWF)."[9] The IWF is an industry-created consortium that lobbies on behalf on Internet providers. "Its activities concentrate on usenet discussion groups, and the organization acts upon Internet user reports."[10] After questionable content is found, the IWF notifies its members and appropriate law enforcement agencies, which then take any relevant legal action. There are pluses and minuses to the IWF. On the downside is that the user must be motivated to call the hotline. Typically those who complain are individuals or well-funded groups with strong religious or moral beliefs. They do not represent the average Internet user or surfer.

Filtering. Web site content filtering and blocking settings are standard features in most Web browsers. In the "Tools" section of Internet Explorer, for example, it is possible to prevent users (such as children) from accessing certain kinds of content. Mozilla Firefox has a similar capability. Users often have the option to do this by blocking Web sites with certain content or specifying approved Web sites. There are also companies such as WebSafety Inc. that sell this kind of product to consumers.

Rating systems. Another mechanism for dealing with inappropriate content is through rating systems. These can be determined either by the content publisher, such as a video game company or Web content provider, or by a neutral third party. For example, http://www.safesurf.com has a rating system that provides Internet users with a number to indicate how appropriate a Web site's content is before a user enters. However, these sorts of capabilities slow down the Internet users' experience.

Regulation. Regulation is another option. This would include that Internet Servicer Providers and content providers voluntarily submit to inspection under mutually agreed upon rules and standards monitored by a government agency or other group.

Proper training of employees. Given that social engineering is one of the most dominant ways that cybercriminals get access to computer systems, perhaps a case can be made to better train criminal justice practitioners and company employees so they are not susceptible to the techniques of cybercriminals.

CONFRONTING CYBERCRIME

Those responsible for dealing with cybercrime must not let public panic and politics get the best of them. They need to make decisions based on empirical evidence and common sense. Yet many people decide to ignore warning signs. These are often the same individuals who are typically victimized by cybercriminals.

This book is an introduction to the world of cybercrime. It reviews the most dominant types and well-publicized cybercrimes, their perpetrators, and some famous cases. The discussion also examines the problems of responding to the cybercrime threat. No prevention and detection mechanism is foolproof. A relatively tech-savvy child can get around the filtering and blocking system that some parents install on their home computers. That is why people must be constantly vigilant to protect against violations of privacy and security, which are too often taken for granted. People must be wary of quick technological fixes that seem obsolete no sooner than they are installed or downloaded.

Chronology

1969 ARPANET is developed.

1980 Bulletin Board Services (BBS) are invented.

1983 First publicly known act of computer hacking is detected when the mainframes of Sloan-Kettering Cancer Center and Los Alamos National Laboratory reveal unauthorized entrance into their computer systems.

1986 Federal government passes Computer Fraud and Abuse Act designed to deter unauthorized access to federal computers.

1988 In November 1988 Robert Morris Jr., a student at Cornell University and the son of the chief scientist for the U.S. National Computer Security Center, releases one of the very first Internet worms. Machines infected by the worm slow down, until they no longer work.

1989 Antinuclear hackers, whose identities have not been confirmed, launch the WANK worm. WANK, the acronym for Worms Against Nuclear Killers, only affects computers made by the now-defunct DEC Corporation. It is sent to protest a NASA space probe that had nuclear materials.

1990 U.S. Department of Justice, Bureau of Justice Statistics produces first study of victimization of corporations and public universities by cybercrime.

1991 The Michelangelo virus, which was programmed to activate on March 6, 1992, is discovered. Once activated, the virus had the ability to shut down a computer, so the machine would not turn on and any data on the computer would be overwritten.

1994 David LaMacchia, a student at the Massachusetts Institute of Technology, starts making copyrighted software available for free through a BBS. Shortly thereafter LaMacchia is arrested by the FBI and charged with attempting to commit wire fraud.

1995 Tsutomu Shimomura, physics engineer and computer security expert, helps the FBI detect and capture cybercriminal Kevin Mitnick.

1996 University of California, Irvine, student Richard Machado sends hate e-mail threatening to kill other students. He is eventually arrested, charged, and convicted of violating his victims' civil rights. Machado becomes the first person in the United States convicted in federal courts of using the Internet to harass others. The same year the federal government passes the Communications Decency Act (CDA), the first notable attempt by the U.S. Congress to monitor pornography on the Internet.

1997 The Supreme Court partially overturns the Communications Decency Act (CDA) because the legislation impinged on the constitutionally protected right to free speech.

1997 Phreakers in New York City break in to the New York City Police Department call center system. They replace the official message with one instructing callers that the police are too busy eating donuts and drinking coffee to respond to their calls.

1999 Shawn Fanning, a teenager from Brockton, Massachusetts, develops a computer program called Napster that can be downloaded from the Internet for free. Napster allows users to share music and other types of files across the Internet. The popularity of the site eventually leads to widespread piracy and legal action from copyright holders.

2000 Popular search engine Yahoo! is subjected to a denial-of-service (DOS) attack. Users with Yahoo! e-mail accounts are prohibited from using them for approximately three hours.

2000 Philippino computer student Onel De Guzman launches the ILOVEYOU virus.

2001 The USA PATRIOT Act is passed. The legislation significantly enables the U.S. government to search its citizens e-mail communications and thus reduced constitutionally mandated provisions on Americans' right to privacy.

2001 In May, FBI investigators file charges for credit card fraud, bank fraud, and other online fraud totaling an estimated $117 million against almost 100 individuals and businesses as part of Operation CyberLoss. By July the Red Code virus, which defaced Web sites and left the message "hacked by the Chinese," infects close to 250,000 computers, prompting fears by government officials that it would slow the Internet when it re-emerged on August 1.

2002 Kevin Mitnick, a self-confessed former hacker who was convicted of several computer crimes, writes a book, *The Art of Deception*.

2002 U.S. Veterans' Administration Medical Center in Indianapolis sells its outdated desktop computers. Later it is discovered that the VA did not adequately remove important personal and credit-related information contained on the computers.

2003 13-year-old Ryan Patrick Halligan hangs himself after being subjected to repeated instant messages (IM) and Internet bullying.

2004 European Economic Union establishes ENISA, a regional agency that is responsible for coordinating investigations into cybercrime by police in member countries and disseminating information about threats.

2006 13-year-old Megan Meier commits suicide after Lori Drew, the mother of one of Meier's former friends, posed as a 16-year-old boy named Josh Evans and created a fake MySpace account under his name. Numerous people in Meier's circle of acquaintances contributed negative posts.

Endnotes

Introduction

1. Frank Schmalleger. *Criminal Justice: A Brief Introduction,* 6th ed. (Upper Saddle River, NJ: Prentice Hall, 2006), 64.
2. Samuel C. McQuade III. *Understanding and Managing Cybercrime.* (Boston: Allyn & Bacon/Pearson, 2006), 2.
3. Ibid., 3.
4. Gina De Angelis. *Cyber Crimes.* (Philadelphia, Pa.: Chelsea House, 2000), 24.
5. Majid Yar. *Cybercrime and Society.* (London: Sage Publications, 2006), 8.
6. David S. Wall. *Cybercrime: The Transformation of Crime in the Information Age.* (Cambridge: Polity Press, 2007), 207–208.
7. McQuade, *Understanding and Managing Cybercrime,* 16–17.
8. Yar, *Cybercrime and Society,* 8.

Chapter 1

1. McQuade, *Understanding and Managing Cybercrime,* 78.
2. Yar, *Cybercrime and Society,* 8.
3. Ibid., 13.
4. McQuade, *Understanding and Managing Cybercrime,* 129.
5. Schmalleger, *Criminal Justice: A Brief Introduction,* 65.

6. Wall, *Cybercrime: The Transformation of Crime in the Information Age,* 53.
7. Michael Levi, "Between the risk and the reality falls the shadow evidence and urban legends in computer fraud (with apologies to T.S. Eliot)," in *Crime and the Internet,* ed. David S. Wall (London: Routledge, 2001), 46.
8. David S. Wall, "Cybercrime, Media and Insecurity: The Shaping of Public Perceptions of Cybercrime," *International Review of Law, Computers and Technology* 22, No. 1–2 (2008): 47.
9. McQuade, *Understanding and Managing Cybercrime,* 48.
10. Yar, *Cybercrime and Society,* 26–27.
11. Ibid., 126.
12. Ibid., 176.
13. Ibid., 190.

Chapter 2

1. Paul Taylor, "Hacktivism: In Search of Lost Ethics," in *Crime and the Internet,* ed. David S. Wall (London: Routledge, 2001), xi, 59–73.
2. Yar, *Cybercrime and Society,* 33; Paul Taylor, "Hacktivism: In Search of Lost Ethics," in *Crime and the Internet,* ed.

David S. Wall (London: Routledge, 2001), 59–73, 66.

3. Yar, *Cybercrime and Society,* 33–34.

4. Ibid., 35.

5. Wall, *Cybercrime: The Transformation of Crime in the Information Age,* 54.

6. Ibid., 55.

7. Ibid., 55–56.

8. McQuade, *Understanding and Managing Cybercrime,* 115.

9. Yar, *Cybercrime and Society,* 47.

10. McQuade, *Understanding and Managing Cybercrime,* 98.

11. Ibid., 65.

12. Ibid., 100.

13. Ibid., 100.

14. Ibid., 65.

15. Taylor, "Hacktivism: In Search of Lost Ethics," 66.

16. McQuade, *Understanding and Managing Cybercrime,* 126.

17. George C. Smith, "The Little Virus That Didn't," *Washington Journalism Review* (May 1992).

18. Wall, *Cybercrime: The Transformation of Crime in the Information Age,* 62–64.

19. Ibid., 65.

20. Ibid., 68.

21. Alex P. Schmid, 1983. *Political terrorism: A research guide to concepts, theories, data bases and literature* (New Brunswick, N.J.: Transaction Publishers, 1983), 111.

22. Jeffrey Ian Ross, *Political Terrorism: An Interdisciplinary Approach* (New York: Peter Lang, 2007), 8.

23. Yar, *Cybercrime and Society,* 55.

Chapter 3

1. McQuade, *Understanding and Managing Cybercrime,* 87.

2. David S. Wall, *Cybercrime: The Transformation of Crime in the Information Age* (Cambridge: Polity Press, 2007), 98.

3. *Ibid.,* 99.

4. McQuade, *Understanding and Managing Cybercrime,* 87.

5. International Intellectual Property Alliance, "Copyright and Trade Issues," IIPA. Available online. URL: http://www.iipa.com/copyright-trade_issues.html. Accessed on February 23, 2009.

6. Wall, *Cybercrime: The Transformation of Crime in the Information Age,* 98.

7. Lundsford, Dale L., and Walter A. Robbins, "Cyber-Criminals and Data Sanitization: A Role for Forensic Accountants," *The Forensic Examiner* (Summer 2005): 50–54.

8. Ibid., 51.

9. Ibid., 51.

Chapter 4

1. McQuade, *Understanding and Managing Cybercrime,* 71.

2. Wall, *Cybercrime: The Transformation of Crime in the Information Age,* 78.

3. Ibid, 76.

Chapter 5

1. Louise Ellison, "Cyberstalking: Tackling Harassment on

the Internet," in *Crime and the Internet*, ed. David S. Wall (London: Routledge, 2001), 141–151.

2. Ibid., 141.
3 McQuade, *Understanding and Managing Cybercrime*, 95.
4. Ellison, "Cyberstalking: Tackling Harassment on the Internet." 146.
5. Ibid., 147.
6. Wall, *Cybercrime: The Transformation of Crime in the Information Age*, 125.
7. Laura Nielsen, "Subtle, Pervasing, Harm: Racist and Sexist Remarks in Public as Hate Speech, *Journal of Social Issues* 58, no. 2 (2002): 266.

Chapter 6

1. Wall, *Cybercrime: The Transformation of Crime in the Information Age*, 6.
2. Ibid, 110.
3. Ibid, 110.
4. Keith Sharpe and Sarah Earle, "Cyberpunters and Cyberwhores: Prostitution on the Internet," In *Dot.cons: Crime, Deviance and Identity on the Internet*, ed. Yvonne Jewkes (Devon, U.K.: Willan Publishing, 2002), 36–52.

Chapter 7

1. The White House. *Defending America's Cyberspace:*

National Plan for Information Systems Protection. (2000) Available online. URL: http://www.fas.org/irp/offdocs/pdd/CIP-plan.pdf. Downloaded on April 10, 2009.

2. Yar, *Cybercrime and Society*, 93–94.
3. Charles Welford, "Preface," in *Understanding and Managing Cybercrime*, ed. Samuel C. McQuade III (Boston: Allyn & Bacon/Pearson, 2006), x–xi.
4. Jack Jacobia, "Computer Forensics: Duties of the first responder," *Law Enforcement Technology* 31, no. 4, (April 2004): 28.
5. Yar, *Cybercrime and Society*, 16–17.
6. Peter Grabosky, and Russell Smith, "Telecommunication fraud in the digital age: the consequence of technologies," in *Crime and the Internet*, ed. David S. Wall (London: Routledge, 2001), 29
7. Yar, *Cybercrime and Society*, 40.
8. McQuade, *Understanding and Managing Cybercrime*, 18.
9. Yaman Akdeniz, "Controlling illegal and harmful content on the Internet," in *Crime and the Internet*, ed. David S. Wall (London: Routledge, 2001), 122.
10. Ibid., 122.

Glossary

application   Another term for software.

BBS   Acronym for Bulletin Board System. BBS allows computer users to communicate with each other through a computer and modem and telephone wire. This kind of system bypasses the need to use the Internet. Its use was more prominent before the growth of the Internet.

cracker   A person who enters a computer system illegally in order to damage it.

e-zine   An electronic or online magazine.

hacker   A person who illegally gains access to a computer system in order to view its contents and is motivated by the thrill of accomplishing this task.

hardware   The actual computer, router, PDA, or cell phone.

Internet   A network that joins computer users, enabling them to communicate and share information. This is facilitated through a complex system of fiber-optic cables, routers, switches, and satellites, which are disproportionately owned by major communication companies.

Internet Service Provider (ISP)   Business or organization that carries the signals for Internet communication.

modem   A mechanism that allows a computer to gain access to the Internet.

operating system   The structure or architecture of internal commands that allow software to run.

phreaks, phone phreaks, and phreakers   Individuals who obtained illegal access via the telephone to wreak havoc on companies and organizations. They have predominantly been replaced by hackers and crackers.

router   A switching box that enables different computers to be connected to the Internet.

search engine   Allows computer users to browse the Web, to find Internet addresses and the information that accompanies them.

server   A large mainframe computer.

social engineering   Obtaining critical information about an organization's computer system by covertly posing as a confidant or insider.

software Computer programs that contain applications such as word processing, statistical analysis, publishing, and e-mail.

wireless Allows computer users to access the Internet without having to attach their computer to a USB cable.

World Wide Web Allows for the transmission of texts, images, and videos from one computer to another.

Bibliography

Acdeniz, Yaman. "Controlling illegal and harmful content on the Internet." In *Crime and the Internet*, edited by David S. Wall, 113–140. London: Routledge, 2001.

Campbell-Kelly, Martin and William Aspray. *Computer: A History Of The Information Machine*, 2d ed. Boulder, Colo.: Westview Press, 2004.

De Angelis, Gina. *Cyber Crimes*. Philadelphia, Pa.: Chelsea House, 2000.

Ellison, Louise. "Cyberstalking: Tackling Harassment on the Internet." In *Crime and the Internet*, edited by David S. Wall, 141–151. London: Routledge, 2001.

Grabosky, Peter. "Virtual Criminology: Old Wine in New Bottles?" *Social and Legal Studies* 10, 1 (2001): 243–249.

IIPA (International Intellectual Property Alliance)."Copyright and Trade Issues," IIPA. Available online. URL: http://www.iipa.com/copyrighttrade_issues.html. Accessed on February 23, 2009.

Jacobia, Jack. "Computer Forensics: Duties of the first responder," *Law Enforcement Technology* 31, 4 (April 2004): 28–34.

Lundsford, Dale L., and Walter A. Robbins. "Cyber-Criminals and Data Sanitization: A Role for Forensic Accountants," *The Forensic Examiner* (Summer 2005): 50–54.

McQuade, Samuel C. III. *Understanding and Managing Cybercrime*. Boston: Allyn & Bacon/Pearson, 2006.

Middleton, Bruce. *Cybercrime Investigators Field Guide*. 2d ed. Boca Raton, Fla.: Averbach Publications, 2005.

Miller, Roger Leroy, ed. *Current Perspectives: Readings from InfoTrac College Edition: Cybercrime*. Belmont, Calif.: Cengage, 2006.

Mitnick, K.D., and W.A. Simon. *The Art of Deception: Controlling the Human Element in Security*. Indianapolis, Ind.: Wiley Publishing, 2002.

Mitnick, K.D., and W.A. Simon. *The Art of Intrusion: The Real Stories Behind the Exploits of Hackers, Intruders, and Deceivers*. Indianapolis, Ind.: Wiley Publishing, 2005.

Parker, Donn. *Crime by Computer*. New York: Scribners, 1976.

Parker, Donn. *Fighting Computer Crime: A New Framework for Protecting Information*. New York: John Wiley & Sons, 1998.

Ross, Jeffrey Ian. *Political Terrorism: An Interdisciplinary Approach.* New York: Peter Lang Publishing, 2007.

Schmalleger, Frank, and Michael Pittaro, eds. *Crimes of the Internet.* Upper Saddle River, N.J.: Pearson, 2008.

Schmid, Alex. *Political Terrorism: A Research Guide to Concepts, Theories, Data Bases and Literature.* New Brunswick, N.J.: Transaction Publishers, 1983.

Sharpe, Keith, and Sarah Earle. "Cyberpunters and Cyberwhores: Prostitution on the Internet." In *Dot.cons: Crime, Deviance and Identity on the Internet*, edited by Yvonne Jewkes, 36–52, Devon, U.K.: Willan Publishing, 2002.

Sterling, Bruce. *The Hacker Crackdown: Law and Disorder on the Electronic Frontier.* New York: Penguin, 1994.

Taylor, Paul. "Hacktivism: In Search of Lost Ethics." In *Crime and the Internet*, edited by David S. Wall, 59–73. London: Routledge, 2001.

United States. 2000. *Defending America's Cyberspace: National Plan for Information Systems Protection.* Available online. URL: http://www.fas.org/irp/offdocs/pdd/CIP-plan.pdf downloaded on April 10, 2009.

United States Bureau of Justice Statistics. *Cybercrime Against Business: Pilot Test Results. 2001 Computer Security Study.* Washington, D.C.: U.S. Department of Justice, 2004.

Wall, David S., ed. *Crime and the Internet.* London: Routledge, 2001.

Wall, David S. "Maintaining order and law on the Internet." In *Crime and the Internet*, edited by David S. Wall, 167–183. London: Routledge, 2001.

Wall, David S. *Cybercrime: The Transformation of Crime in the Information Age.* Cambridge: Polity Press, 2007.

Wall, David S. "Cybercrime and the Culture of Fear: Social Science Fiction(s) and the Production of Knowledge about Cybercrime." *Information, Communication & Society* 11, 6 (2008): 861–884.

Wall, David S. "Cybercrime, Media and Insecurity: The Shaping of Public Perceptions of Cybercrime." *International Review of Law, Computers and Technology* 22, 1–2 (2008): 45–63.

Welford, Charles. "Preface." In *Understanding and Managing Cybercrime*, edited by Samuel C. McQuade III, x–xi. Boston: Allyn & Bacon/Pearson, 2006.

Yar, Majid. *Cybercrime and Society.* London: Sage Publications, 2006.

Index

About the Author

Jeffrey Ian Ross, Ph.D., is an associate professor in the Division of Criminology, Criminal Justice, and Forensic Studies, and a Fellow of the Center for International and Comparative Law at the University of Baltimore. He has researched, written, and lectured on national security, political violence, political crime, violent crime, corrections, and policing for over two decades. He is the author, co-author, editor, and co-editor of 13 books. Ross has performed consulting services for Westat, CSR, U.S. Department of Defense, United States Department of Justice (USDOJ): Office of Juvenile Justice and Delinquency Prevention, USDOJ: National Institute of Justice; U.S. Department of Homeland Security, and Intel Science Talent Search. From 1995–1998, Ross was a social science analyst with the National Institute of Justice, a division of the U.S. Department of Justice. In 2003, he was awarded the University of Baltimore's Distinguished Chair in Research award. His Web site is http://www.jeffreyianross.com.

About the Consulting Editor

John L. French is a 31-year veteran of the Baltimore City Police Crime Laboratory. He is currently a crime laboratory supervisor. His responsibilities include responding to crime scenes, overseeing the preservation and collection of evidence, and training crime scene technicians. He has been actively involved in writing the operating procedures and technical manual for his unit and has conducted training in numerous areas of crime scene investigation. In addition to his crime scene work, Mr. French is also a published author, specializing in crime fiction. His short stories have appeared in *Alfred Hitchcock's Mystery Magazine* and numerous anthologies.